D1287666

Sharing Our Stories: A Hospice Whispers Grief Support Workbook

Front cover initial image by Amy Kappler hipposeatingalligators.com
Front cover art by Laura Saintey acrylic painting.
Front cover graphic design by Laura Jenkins storyscape.com

Permission Granted by Janie Cook for use of all her poems and quotes available at livingwiththelossofachild.blogspot.com/

Cataloging-in Publication Data

Carla Cheatham
Sharing Our Stories: A Hospice Whispers Grief Support Workbook

I. Grief support	II. Bereavement support	III. Hospice Care	IV. Palliative Care
R 726.8		362.175 CH	

ISBN: 978-0-9966010-1-6

Sharing Our Stories:
A Hospice Whispers Grief Support Workbook

by Rev. Dr. Carla Cheatham

PRAISE FOR
Sharing Our Stories:
A Hospice Whispers Grief Support Workbook
AND AUTHOR CARLA CHEATHAM

Sharing Our Stories: A Hospice Whispers Grief Support Workbook is a wonderful gift— a beautifully constructed book that includes inspiration and opportunities for reflection. Individuals who are experiencing loss will find much in this sensitive workbook to help them marshal their resources to cope with grief.

Kenneth J Doka, PhD
Author, *Grief is a Journey: Finding Your Path Through Loss*

In an invitation to explore the contours and gifts of our grief, this companion to *Hospice Whispers* escorts us safely along a course of reflection. Here we can record the spoken and unspoken experiences of our own lives as we accompany the dying and those who love them. Wisdom and growth are the products of this work. Thank you, Rev. Carla Cheatham for guiding us!

Monica Williams-Murphy, MD
Huntsville Hospital Emergency Physician & Medical Director, Advanced Care Planning & End-of-Life Education
National Speaker, Award-Winning Writer, Author of *"It's OK to Die"- An End of Life Planning Guide*

As a powerful companion workbook to *Hospice Whispers: Stories of Life, Sharing Our Stories: A Hospice Whispers Grief Support Workbook* deepens our awareness of our unique grief, it helps us to discover how to ask for the support we need in our grieving journey, and guides us to a place where we can come to terms with the death of our loved one(s). This workbook is for the grieving family, grieving friends or the solitary griever. Whether your grief has just begun or is decades old, this thoughtful resource is a gentle path towards healing.

Barbara Karnes, RN
Award winning End of Life Educator and Hospice Pioneer

Sharing Our Stories offers a well-written, much needed guide through being with, and supporting those of us who are living and working with death and dying. On a personal level, it offered me a gentle hand to hold during the last days of two people very dear to me.

Pamela D. Blair, Ph.D., Interfaith Minister
Author of the bestselling, award winning classic on grief,
I Wasn't Ready to Say Goodbye

During the years of my mother's progressive dementia, I reached for books to help me understand, to give me support, but also to cope with the disillusionment and deep sadness that was encircling me. I knew my mother would die, but I didn't know when (of course) and I didn't know how. I wanted real words, not just hints and euphemisms, not what you see in the movies and on television about dying. I found *Hospice Whispers* by Rev. Dr. Carla Cheatham, and felt like I had a friend, someone to accompany me as I sat with my mother who wanted so much to leave this world. And now, Dr. Cheatham has written a companion workbook called *Sharing our Stories* to help explore our feelings – on our own, with friends and family, or in a support group setting. This workbook is not a cookie cutter approach to grieving, but a sensitive, exploratory book to help us each find our own way when someone we love dies.

Linda Jo Stern, MPH

When you are grieving, you don't want to be alone. If you are looking for someone to quietly guide the steps in healing your grief, I hope you give Rev. Dr. Carla Cheatham's *Hospice Whispers* a chance. With brief glimpses of people she has met in her work as a hospice chaplain, each short chapter will be like holding a helpful hand. *Sharing Our Stories*, the new workbook linked to *Hospice Whispers*, adds depth and practical suggestions for healing. As someone who has led numerous grief support groups for hospice, I enthusiastically recommend these books as a great resource.

Rev. Larry Patten, Hospice Bereavement Support Specialist
Fresno, California

Grief is universal; grieving is not. Every person's journey through grief is unique. Grieving is not a one-size-fits-all type of process, and in her book, *Sharing Our Stories: A Hospice Whispers Grief Support Workbook*, Carla captures not only the shared experience of grief, but also encourages her readers to embark on their own individualistic grief journey in order to find a sense of healing and a new norm after the devastating loss of a loved one. Her workbook differs from other grief workbooks, as the questions that are asked are very real, very thought-provoking, and very healing as emotions are recognized and processed through the utilization of this workbook. Some of the questions raised are hard to consider...but grief work IS hard and the things presented to the reader for their consideration in this workbook will offer the reader a chance to think carefully about the in-depth questions that we who grieve wish someone...anyone...would ask so that our healing can begin.

Bonnie Camp, MSW, LSW, CT, GC-C
Social Worker and Grief Support Specialist

For those of us who are grief-workers, finding a voice as clear and engaging as Rev. Dr. Carla Cheatham's is rare. When that voice offers tidings of wisdom and truth, hope and humor as she addresses grief and its inevitable obstacles, it is almost a miracle. Yet these are the powerful yet accessible messages that are found in Carla's latest work, *Sharing Our Stories,* a workbook for the grieving that is a companion piece to her iconic work *Hospice Whispers* of 2014.

For anyone who is grieving and who feels isolated and unsure how to move the process forward, or for grief counselors, social workers, psychologists, and chaplains who are the companions to those who grieve, this workbook provides an abundance of ways to help. There are thoughtful poems, quotes and journaling prompts, but more importantly, there is room for those using the workbook to find their own pace and comfort level.

I am very much looking forward to using this splendid resource both in group settings and with individual clients.

Deb Wojcik, MSW, LCSW
Bereavement Coordinator, Cancer Wellness Center
Psychotherapist in private practice

Prepare to read *Hospice Whispers* and the accompanying *Sharing Our Stories* workbook with tears in your eyes. Articulate, gracious, and humbling—these stories will resonate with readers, while the workbook provides a safe place to pour out that grief-seared resonance. An excellent resource that will assist the bereaved as they cope with their own grief journey, and serve as a tool to aid pastors, grief counselors, and others as they minister to the grief-stricken. Well done by a hospice chaplain who has accompanied many through the morass of grief and bereavement.

Cherie Fry, PhD, BCCC, CT, CFHPC
Hospice Chaplain

Carla Cheatham has an intimate story-telling style that invites the reader into her experiences with families who are caring for loved ones who are dying. Through her stories she reveals her sensitivity to the emotions, struggles and needs that grief creates. She demonstrates the compassionate love that opens the way for people in sorrow to find comfort, humor and hope.

This book is a great resource for families who are caring for their terminally ill loved ones, for friends who want to help others who are grieving and for all positions on both hospice and hospital staffs.

Carla does not lecture, does not give a 1,2,3 way of caring for someone who is dying . . . instead she tenderly describes each person, their unique needs and then shares her heartfelt instinct in trusting her compassionate sense of what will ease the tension in the room. She gives us an elegantly beautiful image of what the end of life can be.

Janie Cook
Grief Group Facilitator
Bereaved parent

Discovery and recovery come to those who have courage to embrace an intimate relationship with grief. I encourage you to take the healing journey with Carla, through *Sharing Our Stories: A Hospice Whispers Grief Support Workbook*. With sensitivity and transparency, Carla skillfully draws a rare form of wisdom from a colorful pallet of seasoned grievers. This workbook is an invaluable resource for both professionals and the bereft.

Linda Vogel
Director of Family Care, TriCare Hospice
Advanced Practice Palliative Care Chaplain and Palliative Life Coach

This workbook is dedicated to:

those who have walked with death, found new life, and graciously allowed me to share their journey…

those who have sat with me in the midst of my own grief until I could be with it myself…

and each of you who have helped me find the embers of meaning and new life in the darkest nights of the soul, encouraged me to fan them into bright flame, and lovingly challenged me to share them with others…

It remains my greatest gift and deepest honor to share this journey with each of you.

For M.G.

For filling in, helping me fill up, and lighting my way home, "piece by peace."

For K.R.

For being present with me so I could be present with myself, and for giving me so many words to claim now as my own, then pass on to others.

For S.B.

For consistently practicing with me, in the healthiest of ways.

For C.H.

For always being a solid place to land, then take flight again, even higher.

I love each of you and, because of you,
I can love "me", and others, even more.

~Namaste~

Table of Contents

Preface

When I first published *Hospice Whispers: Stories of Life* in 2014, I assumed that people who were grieving would avoid stories about the end of life like the plague. Thankfully, I was wrong. I had forgotten how helpful it can be to hear others' experiences, reactions, and ways of understanding when we are in the midst of our own pain.

I received calls and messages from numerous people who had experienced grief over the death of a loved one, describing ways in which the stories from the book had helped them process their own grief and stories.

One woman, midway through reading *Hospice Whispers*, e-mailed me to say she just had to put the book down and contact me to thank me, "for encouraging people to use the real words" for death and dying. She went on to say:

> "When I use the real words, it makes others uncomfortable, but when I try to use the words that are easier for them to hear about my daughter's death, it makes ME squirm. I may 'pass' a cup. I might 'lose' a sock. But not my daughter. My daughter died! Thank you for validating this for me."

Another reader, a hospice nurse, shared that she excitedly opened her Kindle once she got on a plane after a conference, intending to relax and enjoy the book on her flight home.

> "So I'm reading along and getting a little misty-eyed because I'm touched by the experiences you have with patients who so openly share their journey with you. It's how I like to practice nursing, so it really spoke to me.
>
> But then I got to the point in the story 'What Better Place' where the daughter says, 'What better place is there for my momma than right here beside me?', and I absolutely lost it!
>
> You see, I'm still angry at my sister and best friend for dying months apart a couple of years ago and leaving me behind, and I didn't realize that grief was still there. That line just burst open the flood gates and I started doing what Oprah calls 'the ugly cry'."

By now, the nurse was laughing as she continued her story:

> "It wasn't pretty! My seatmate was worried about me, the flight attendant checked on me…it was so bad I had to stop reading until I got home. And even then, I'm sitting in bed next to my husband reading it before going to sleep, and I started that ugly cry again. So now my husband was worried about me!"

I laughed along with her but was also truly half-concerned when I asked if I should apologize for this being her experience.

> "Oh, NO!" she said, still laughing, "It was exactly what I needed because I know I need to get it out so I can move on, and your stories helped me do that. It just became really comical that I had to be careful when and where I read it because I learned that whenever I did, more grief would come tumbling out.
>
> It was really quite a gift for me, and I'm so grateful. I needed to tell you all of this because I figured you would get it; you could understand."

Those who've experienced grief usually can. One reader contacted me with the following:

> "This is the first thing I've been able to stand reading in the four years since [my loved one] died that didn't make me want to scream, cuss, throw it across the room, vomit, or all of the above. You're the first person who doesn't seem to need to 'fix' me. You can just let me be where I am and give me the space to know that it's completely okay for me to be there and you're okay with it.
>
> I haven't found that anywhere else, and I desperately needed some place for my feelings to be okay and accepted. As soon as I started reading your book, I felt that freedom and something relaxed inside of me in a way I've not experienced since she died."

Another person shared:

> "There are some things that I couldn't come to terms with about my father before he died, and it's haunted me. Several stories in the book helped me make sense out of a lot of things that happened in my family as he died. They [The *Hospice Whispers* stories] helped me feel less guilty about still being pissed off at someone who, suddenly, everybody in my family was talking about as if he had been a saint! Thank you for that. It helped me understand the whole situation a lot more and made me feel much less alone."

The stories of healing continued to come, until it was clear that this workbook must be written to provide guidance and support to *Hospice Whispers* readers as they re-experienced their own tales of grief and sought meaning for it all. What began as a short list of questions for each story grew as both bereaved and professionals asked for more.

I don't know your story. I don't know what your experience with death was (or is) like or what grieving is like for you now. I'm uncertain how the 38 stories from the original book, and the reflection questions based upon them that follow in this workbook, may effect you.

Wherever you are in your grief, and however the *Sharing Our Stories: A Hospice Whispers Grief Support Workbook* impacts you, my greatest hope is that you find some sense of being less alone in your grief—more understood—and that this work might help you process your own stories in a way that brings healing, freedom, and hope.

Where it meets these goals—I am grateful. Where it misses the mark—I ask your forgiveness. In either case, I hope you will share feedback with me at hospicewhispers.com and explore additional reflection questions, information about grief, theories of grief, and other resources available there.

Ultimately, I trust you to find your way, find new meaning, and find a little renewed peace over time as you slowly adjust to this path you never chose. As you are finding your way, please remember: you are not alone.

Peace to you,
Carla

About the Quotes and Poems in This Workbook

I have found in my practice, and in my own life, that when we are in the depths of grappling with raw emotion and are trying to come to terms with the unimaginable, clear thinking can temporarily elude us. There is too much to process and so much emotion that our concentration, memory, and focus may be greatly impaired for a period of time.

Short, simple words and phrases that speak directly to our grief can be life preservers onto which we can cling when the waters are at their most overwhelming.

They let us know that others truly do understand what we are feeling because, in some capacity, they have been there, too. They can give us hope that perhaps we will feel less broken someday and that the crashing of grief over our heads will not always drown out the sounds of beauty and calm.

Therefore, I have included a large number of quotes in this workbook that I hope will be of comfort to you. Some may speak to you; others may not ring true; some may unintentionally hit a raw nerve and inspire anger.

As with all portions of this book, take what you like and leave the rest. Please keep in mind if you do find quotes and poems meaningful and wish to share them to provide proper credit to the authors and obtain any necessary permission based on copyright laws.

Many of the poems were contributed by friend and colleague, Janie Cook, and are shared with her gracious permission. Janie and her husband have two children—a son and a daughter—and live in Austin, Texas. Their son, Matt, died of depression through suicide that claimed his life in 2007.

They experienced the sudden death of a child and the complicated grief that persons experience when society heaps stigmas born of ignorance and fear on the families of those who make this choice. It broke their hearts, but also broke their souls open to greater compassion, love, and understanding.

It led Janie to begin working as a facilitator of grief groups and to share her experience with others who are mourning, especially after the death of a child, through her blog at livingwiththelossofachild.blogspot.com.

Again, many thanks to Janie, and others, whose words are shared throughout this text.

Not a Loss

This morning
bathed in the light of this new day
with its sparkling, glittering, quiet newness
it comes to me that Matt's death is not a loss
 but a difference.

I feel him so strongly
his spirit shining more brightly each day
as he grows into his new existence
 learning to breathe the light
 travel with the wind
 sing each bird song
 greet me in each flower
and surprise me over and over with brilliance.

We haven't lost him . . . we must simply learn a new way to be together

And once we do that, this will be so much easier
 less tangled
 less fractured
 less anxious
 less dependent upon the physical and the temporal

My tears change
 sometimes they don't come from sadness
 but from the joy of Truth.

- Janie Cook

How To Use This Workbook

The Many Expressions of Grief

We often speak in terms of a grief journey, as if there is a hypothetical endpoint we will reach. Even theoretical models intended to help us understand and explain what happens through grief use words such as "tasks" or "stages" or the "process" of grief, as if there is something we are required to complete or overcome in order to be happy again.

(A summary of some of these grief models, along with a list of resources such as websites, books, articles, and videos related to grief and the process of bereavement can be found on my website at hospicewhispers.com)

I may use these words, as well, because language is, at times, limited. It is not my intention to imply that there is a destination to get to, an end in sight, or that this workbook will help you get there and be done with grief. I can't in good faith promise you that.

As my friend, Janie Cook, writes:

> "The journey is our story. There is no destination, no resting place to reach, no final answer. There is simply the journey we take and the story we live with our feet, with our heart. We may stop along the way to rest—not because we have arrived, but to take this part in a little more deeply. We may pause to listen or savor a threshold, but the journey is our story, The Story. Each obstacle we overcome, each companion treasured, each grief suffered is a sacred moment along the way."

Grief doesn't necessarily end for everyone. In fact, many would argue that it *never* ends, it just shifts and changes over time and gets a bit easier to live with as we gradually find ways to integrate such a major change into our lives. We find ways to honor the life we miss; hold onto the good memories; make peace with the not-so-good ones; build a new relationship with the person who is no longer physically there; and find ways to continue living our lives.

Often, because our relationships help define us—as grandchild, child, sibling, spouse, parent, friend—we must go through the process of re-imagining our own identity when that person is gone. While all of this is a process, it is far from formulaic. There are no linear, prescribed formulas for what grief should look like.

For example, in one grief group I facilitated, there were people who expressed feeling guilty for crying, while others felt guilt for not. Some grappled with feeling relief, not that their loved one was dead, but that the suffering was over.

Others described survivor guilt—questioning why they are alive when multiple loved ones have died so young, some from disease or accidents and others from trauma in war. By contrast, others questioned why death waited so long and allowed their loved one to suffer for month or years.

Some were there to discuss grief that had just begun. Others were there to cope with the grief they anticipate as dementia or other physical struggles slowly change both the person they know and their world as they know it. Another was just beginning to process the impact of living through a war fought decades ago, and the multitude of traumas he experienced in the midst of daily terror.

As is usual in my work, I heard both the quietly implied and directly stated fears from the participants that they were somehow doing it wrong, a sentiment that was shared no matter where on the grieving spectrum they found themselves. For this group, as with each one I facilitate, the journey begins with listening to one another while validating, normalizing, and affirming feelings and reactions, whatever they may be.

This includes the often heard laughter, which is not an expression of ridicule but of, "Oh yeah, I resemble that remark." Permitting others to express themselves, free of judgment, helps them feel a little less weird and a little less alone.

There is no mid-term, no grade, no evaluation for grief. The only test is whether what a person is doing is working for them. The only wrong thing is that which causes harm to ourselves or to another. Period!

Not everyone in our social circles has experienced grief or learned from the boundaries of a support group. They *may* express judgments born of ignorance, discomfort with witnessing our pain, and a desire for us to hurry up and feel better.

One woman contacted me after reading *Hospice Whispers*, asking for my help. She said she didn't know what was wrong with her, but that everyone was telling her she "should be over it." When I asked her what SHE thought, she replied,

"Well, I should be, shouldn't I? But I'm just not, and I can't make it happen. Then I feel guilty and ashamed and even more alone and angry and misunderstood, which pisses me off even more!"

I responded, "Find places where people can let you just *be*. When you find that, and don't feel rushed, I'm pretty certain you'll notice something loosen inside of you over time. 'Wallow' as long as you need to. In fact, roll around and nest in those feelings as much as you need. When you're done with them, you'll know. Life usually doesn't allow us to stagnate too long, and if we're stuck, we'll eventually know it instinctively from within, not because others are rushing us to move on their timetable.

Feelings need room to move and breathe. When they feel pushed back against, they tighten. When they are given space, they can relax and shift as they need. It will happen naturally, without pushing, from you or anyone else."

in the midst of the beginning

it is the quiet of the moon, shining in the grey blue sky
the brisk, unexpected cool of this August morning
the stillness of daybreak holding its breath
the delicate birdsongs giving birth to a new day

such simple elegance
fills an empty heart
soothes a battered spirit
and allows the spark of gratitude to ignite trust

sitting in the midst of beginning
something tentatively eager opens in me
and I can breathe

~Janie Cook

Certainly, there are cases in which people do get stuck and the natural grief process stalls. In others, the naturally intense feelings of grief can become so magnified that it leads to dysfunction. The body can get caught in a pain loop and need outside assistance, and there is no shame in getting support from a counseling professional when such complicated grief arises.

Places like The Center for Complicated Grief through the Columbia School of Social Work (complicatedgrief.columbia.edu/complicated-grief/) and others can provide more guidance and resources on this topic.

I heard back a few months later from this woman who struggled with her grieving process. She had joined a special yoga class for those who had experienced grief. She laughed,

> "I thought it was ironic that you encouraged me to find a place to let my feelings move and breathe, and then I stumbled into this yoga class completely by accident. I didn't have to explain myself to others in the class because they were there for the same reasons. I could just go in and, well, be!"

I could hear in her voice the very relief she described. It was beautiful. And according to her, it worked to help move her to a new place. And THAT is exactly what I hope this workbook will provide you—a safe space for your feelings to just *be*.

Suggestions for Walking Alone and Sharing with Others

If you choose to go through this workbook alone, allow it to be a tool to learn from your own experiences and also consider others' as described in the book. If you choose to walk through these pages with another person or with a group, use it to help you share your stories, listen to others', swap notes, ask questions, and give yourself and others a lot of safe space to bring in exactly whatever is needed with no judgments.

As grief groups form, each participant steps into the waters of uncertainty and slowly builds the trust necessary to feel comfortable sharing their grief. Over time this may help other people feel more comfortable sharing, as well.

One participant has come to one of my groups for almost a year and does not share. Others have wanted to push, but my job is to remind them of the agreements we make at the beginning of each session, which includes: sharing is optional, not required.

Each person deserves to walk through this experience exactly as they need it to unfold. And so do you. So I encourage you with the following:

1) Take this at your own pace, in your own way. Grief is exhausting. Our brains can consume much more of our bodies' resources (oxygen, nutrients, etc.) when we are mourning, so it can be normal to feel a) like we've run a marathon when we've barely left the couch, and b) like we don't have two brain cells to rub together, much less to read SO many words.

Also, since the circumstances of our grief are unique and our personalities and coping styles differ from person to person, what works for some will not work for another. Not all of the stories or questions below will apply to you or your group, so please adapt as needed. The intent is to go through this workbook in the way that best suits your particular needs.

So skip stories, sections, or questions if you don't have the energy to give or if you're just not feeling it. Pick it up and put it down whenever you need. Talk about what you need to; stay quiet if you don't want to speak. Follow writing prompts if they work for you or blow them off and use the space to write about something else if they don't.

If writing isn't your forte or words are too hard to express right now, use the spaces to draw, collage, or list music lyrics as your way of responding to the prompts. Use the white space to pause and breathe, meditate, repeat a sacred text, or memorized prayer or mantra.

This guide is merely a jumping off point with suggestions about how the stories from the original book may help you process your feelings, clarify your beliefs, and learn more about this human process of dealing with death. Skim the questions and consider them without writing a word, or fill up extra notebooks if I've not given you enough space on the pages.

Since some may be skipping around, some similar questions or themes that arise in different stories have been repeated to make certain they are available to everyone. At the end of the day, take what you like, and leave the rest.

to be alone
with no distractions or demands

to rest deeply
one moment at a time
as long as it takes

to spill my thoughts and feelings onto
the accepting page
and allow the release of that unburdening

to listen and watch without notice of time
and let nature teach me to be at peace
with what is

this is Grace
healing Grace
restoring
renewing
Grace

~Janie Cook

2) Notice any surge of energy that may arise for you in each section. Energy is a point of information. Anger, sadness, fear, etc. are signals that something needs attention. If something elicits a strong response, pause if you can and ask yourself: "Why?" It could be that there's a tender area asking for more reflection or care, or maybe I goofed or was inarticulate in how I presented a scenario or information.

Regardless, try to be kind to yourself about it. Give ample space in your own reflection to let those feelings be acknowledged and find safe spaces to express them with those who understand or are at the least able to listen without trying to tamp that energy down.

3) Please excuse the limitations of language. Throughout this workbook, I use the words "loved one" to refer to whomever it is you may be grieving. However, as I wrote in *Hospice Whispers*, I never assume that one's relationship with a dead or dying friend or family member is or was idyllic and 100% positive.

Your grief process may include struggles related to disconnection, regrets, wounds, etc. My use of the generic term "loved one" does not intend to minimize any hurt you experienced in your relationship or to overstate the positive nature of it or the person. I trust you to find the language that works for you and your individual needs, insert them as substitutions wherever needed, and I hope you will forgive the limitations of language to address all circumstances and relationships.

Also, as I did in the original book of stories, I have chosen to use "G-d" when referencing a deity out of respect and do not intend to assume that this language works for you, either. Again, please insert whatever language makes the most sense for you and your beliefs.

4) Pay attention to whether exploring your story is helping you process and integrate your story or taking you down a rabbit hole. The stories we tell ourselves, and each other, are powerful and have the potential to move us further along or drag us further underwater.

For example, we see the power of story as Bernadette in "The Day of the Dying" shares that her mom, "…was beating herself up, saying she should have said more, should have done this or that. But when she went back to this story…again and again she realized it was all absolutely perfect!"

By sharing and reconsidering the story, Bernadette's mother was able to rewrite the narrative that had been troubling her in her own mind and was able to see the story in a new way that gave her more meaning. Sharing our stories can help us process through exactly this task of reconsidering the story we've been telling ourselves and even finding new meaning in them.

The goal of sharing our stories and considering them on a deeper level is not to rehearse or stay stuck in the emotions of grief or anything that felt negative or challenging about your experience. That type of replay can actually wear a deeper groove into our neural networks, making the memory even more vivid and harder to bear. Certainly we must absolutely tell our stories as long as we need, so long as we are not re-traumatizing ourselves as we do so.

The goal of walking through our stories is to allow us to express our grief, hear others', and find the relief that can come from knowing that what we are feeling and experiencing is not abnormal. When the time is right, we will find ourselves in a less acute, all-consuming place where our sense of loss is no longer quite so overwhelming; it does not dominate every single thought and moment but becomes one part of our lives. That is integration.

While this can be a relief, it can also bring up a new sense of guilt and loss for some, as moving on can feel like we are abandoning the deceased and somehow saying they did not and do not matter. In fact, some bereaved say the second and even third years are harder, as their loss becomes more integrated into their lives and they live in the tension of what was and what life is now seeking to be.

Integrating grief into our lives does not mean that moments do not come; that waves do not still wash over us with a certain song or memory or smell or date. It means that it controls our lives less and less and becomes a part of what actually makes it more sweet, meaningful, and beautiful.

The idea as you approach this workbook is to be clear about anything that may still be hard for you, giving it room to be seen and heard, and then finding a way to make peace with it in whatever way works for you. Sharing our stories, whether we do so with a page or computer screen only or whether we allow others to read or hear them, can help us walk through our feelings, hear ourselves in a different way, and gain a deeper understanding and sense of peace.

But if you find that this process is not accomplishing that for you, do not just push through. Stop the workbook and get support elsewhere. It doesn't mean there's something wrong with you. These pages just may not be the best fit for your personality or where you are on your journey and a different book, workbook, group, or grief counselor may work better for you.

There are stars up above,

So far away that we only see their light long long after the star itself if gone.

And so it is with people that we loved—

Their memories keep shining ever brightly

though their time with us is done.

But the stars that light up the darkest night,

these are the lights that guide us.

As we live our days,

these are the ways we remember."

~Chaim Stern

From the Mishkan T'Filah

(the Jewish Prayer book)

5) Circle the wagons!! As you read and consider the following questions and exercises, please take care of yourself and know that no words on a page can replace in-person support, education, and even professional counsel.

I highly encourage you to walk through this workbook in the company of at least one trusted friend, if not an actual group or professional, who can help you as you find your way. If you choose to work through this text alone, think of a few trusted persons whom you respect and believe would be supportive and helpful listeners if you find you need to talk through whatever comes up for you in the following pages.

Write the names and numbers of those people here as a supportive contact list. It's better to have this list handy well before it is needed. There is nothing like trying to think of names when the brain is fuzzy with feelings or finding phone numbers when eyes are strained by tears.

_____ _____

_____ _____

_____ _____

Think about what you might need from these people. Consider how each one can best be of support to you and which person(s) would be most likely to respond to your particular needs well. Look for persons who can:

1) protect your confidence
2) sit comfortably with you without needing words
3) feel comfortable providing a hand or a hug of comfort if needed/desired
4) listen only without giving feedback, opinions, advice, or trying to fix how you feel
5) be a place to safely bounce off thoughts and ideas without fear of judgment
6) listen and give feedback IF you do ask for that feedback
7) let this be about you and what you need, without inserting their own story unless requested
8) pray or meditate with or for you, if requested
9) other things I've missed _____?

Before you need them, consider contacting this list of people up front with something like the following: "Hey, I'm going to be working through my grief about _____ and I may need _____. Is that something you feel/think you could give?"

If that seems too weird or hard, you may simply choose to be prepared to tell them at the beginning of a call or visit what you most need. For instance, "Please put away the tool belt and hardhat and any need to make this okay for me, and just listen and sit with me in my feelings."

I went through a serious health scare several years ago that put me right into the middle of the healthcare system, but from the other side of the hospital bed. I could not speak to anyone about it for three days. I needed room to process the news—that it might be cancer, multiple organs and issues were involved, and it might be serious—before I could risk speaking of it to anyone else. I didn't have it in me yet to say the words out loud, much less be asked a million questions for which I didn't yet know the answer.

When I finally did tell someone, I chose someone dear to me whom I knew had gone through a similar journey in years past. I asked her, "What do I do?"

Without missing a beat, she said, "Find safe places to cry." It was the single best piece of advice I ever got as I sat through months of tests and uncertainty and grief and fear.

So I did as she suggested: I thought of people I trusted and with whom I felt safe. I also thought of those whom I believed were healthy enough to accept my boundaries, set their own, and truly hear me and respond to what I said I needed, rather than what *they* decided I needed. I also looked for people mature enough to not make this about them, but could keep the focus on me, since that was what I really needed in the heightened and acute stage of my grief and confusion.

It is said that unexpressed expectations are premeditated resentments. So I called. I swallowed hard. I asked:

> "I need a few people whom I can call and ask to come sit beside me, put your arm around me and pat me on the head while I cry, and tell me, 'It's going to be okay.' I won't want you to try to say other things to make me feel better. I probably won't want to talk. Is that something that you have space for right now?"

Most said, "Yes." A couple said no because of other things they had going on in their lives at the time, which meant they had little space to be there for someone else. I didn't take it personally, but appreciated their honesty about what they did and did not have to give! Besides, if I had asked and assumed that they would have agreed, that would have set us both up from the beginning. Asking a "Yes" or "No" question, which has only one answer that I am willing to hear, is not fair.

Those who agreed to be there for me as requested became my safe spaces for the four months of waiting to know what my immediate future held in terms of my health. I only called on them a few times, but just knowing they were there for me felt like a huge safety net, which was always there if I needed it.

When I did call on them, I was clear about what I needed, and I thankfully chose well, because they all responded exactly as I asked. Each time, I sat for maybe 15 minutes. The whole visit always lasted less than an hour. I respected their boundaries and they honored mine.

Scary? Yep. Somewhat embarrassing for this independent woman who falls way too easily into the, "I've got it all together" trap? Oh, HELL yeah! Worth it? Definitely!

It was the best thing I ever could have done for myself during that time. So much so that I found myself wishing that, when I had faced other forms of grief, I had known to follow exactly this process to circle the wagons of support around the open and raw wound of my soul. Not only did it provide me safe space to be with my grief and fear, and have others with me while I sat with it, but it taught me a great deal about holding, and being held.

This may not be for you. The mere thought may have you breaking out in hives and ready to run from this workbook, or simply rolling your eyes and scoffing with a "humph!"

Don't worry! Like everything else in this workbook, it isn't a requirement, but merely an invitation. Do what feels right for you. All I ask is that you please take good, wise, and gentle care of yourself as you explore your grief. You are worth being well-cared for.

Find the process and words that work for you. But do something to circle the wagons around you while considering the *Sharing Our Stories* workbook questions.

6) Lastly, consider whether you want your deceased loved one to join you through this workbook or if you want this space all to yourself. Again, on my website, I briefly cover some of the prevalent theoretical models for grief (hospicewhispers.com). They each have similarities and differences, strengths and weakness, and some professionals and individuals prefer some over others.

One fairly common theme involves finding some new place for the deceased in one's life. To completely compartmentalize them away, as if they never existed or impacted your life, is unrealistic at least and can be harmful at worst. But some partitioning off of our minds and hearts can be adaptive and healthy.

While your deceased loved one is not physically here in person, there is still a new relationship to be developed with the one who is no longer there or the void they have left behind. It's a way of keeping some part of the deceased helpfully with us while also moving forward with life and other relationships in a new and healthy way.

being sad
feeling the loss of a precious smile, the absence of a strong presence
doesn't erase gratitude

struggling to learn to live in a new reality
doesn't overshadow the gift of cherished memories

this is the strange truth
that opposites
like despair and relief
absence and presence
loss and gift
joy and sorrow
can co-exist, conjoined, mysteriously meshed
challenging our tendency to divide reality into distinct parts
redefining clarity and wholeness
and coming to rest deep within
as peace

~Janie Cook

Making the transition of letting go of our loved one's physical presence and leaning more on our memories and our ongoing internal connection to them can take time. There is no replacement for losing access to their smell, their touch, their energy, the many nuances of facial expressions and tone of voice we may know so well. The ache can seem inconsolable.

Some find it helps to develop new ways of being with them and keeping some form of connection with them that feels right. For instance, one man in a grief group I facilitate spoke of missing his wife the most in the mornings when they would normally share a donut and coffee and read the paper.

Realizing that sitting all alone with his grief was not a good long-term solution, he created a new ritual. He now eats his donut, drinks his coffee, and reads his paper on the patio. Friends walk by to say hello (and check on him if he's ever not there!) Over time, the birds, which his wife always loved to watch, began to gather for crumbs.

He says he feels her presence with him there, in those birds, so he gives them a few crumbs at a time from *her* donut. During this time, he smiles in remembrance, talks to her and the birds quietly, and then goes on with his day on his own.

What about you? What are the moments when you miss your loved one the most? Is there a certain event, a certain time of day or week when you would call or visit, a particular struggle you face that they would know just how to handle? Are there new rituals you could develop to help fill that void in a different way, both to keep a connection to them while also building new relationships and continuing your own life?

These questions are important to consider in their own right. But they are also important because you may, or may not, be in the custom of discussing deep or significant things through with your loved one.

If you are accustomed to doing so, you may want to make space to imagine discussing your responses to the questions that follow with them. Others of you may want this space to be completely your own and not include your loved one in it at all.

you are here

in the quiet promise of dawn
in the moment when birds begin their songs
in the agony of painful memories
in the struggle for a new tomorrow
in the reality of empty, hungry arms
in the blessed ability to remember a brilliant smile

when the new depths are cruelly carved
and soul space is created to hold the growing sadness
when spontaneous smiles erupt in new born eyes
washing over my raw places
when new ways of giving myself away are suddenly offered
and wholeness seems like more than just a dream

you are here
you are here

~Janie Cook

Either way is completely fine. It is about what *you* need. If you do decide to include them in the process, you may want to find a certain place, a certain time of day, a certain chair, a certain hiking trail, or mug of coffee or tea to share with them while you imagine talking with them. Whatever you do, continue to follow the, "Do it as long as it's working for you, but stop if it's not" rule of thumb!

My Hope

I hope the stories from *Hospice Whispers*, and the questions and comments I raise around them in this *Sharing Our Stories* workbook, help you as you seek to build a relationship with the one who is no longer here (in person). I hope they will help you see your own story, perhaps in an even more healing and life-giving light. If nothing else, may the pages that follow help reassure you that you are neither weird nor irreparably damaged and that, again, you are definitely not alone.

NOTES FOR FACILITATORS:

"General Questions to Consider" for either journaling or discussion are available through my website at hospicewhispers.com and may be used as warm up questions for individuals or groups to explore their own experience before launching into the stories and workbook.

"Closing Questions to Explore" for either journaling or discussion are available through my website and may be used as a weekly group closing or for a final wrap-up session at the cessation of a group.

For those experiencing Acute Grief, one warm-up question from "General Questions to Consider" followed by the reflection questions from only one story may be a most helpful pace.

For those groups that have been together for some time, are less distracted by the intensity of the initial months of grief, and are looking for other material to explore, they may be better able to handle up to five stories a week for a 90-minute group.

Some facilitators have found it helpful to group stories based on those most appropriate to the type of grief participants are experiencing. For instance, a caregiver support group for persons with Alzheimer's and other dementias may choose to take six weeks to focus on these stories:

"Rachmaninoff"
"A Familiar Tune"
"Of Course You Feel That Way"
"Your Mom Is So Sweet"
"Assuming Mary"
and "Restorying"

Then adding one to three weeks to cover:

"Holding Space"
"To Be Clear"
and "Already Inside You"

For questions related to the use of this workbook, please contact me through hospicewhispers.com

"We light our candle tonight to represent all that brings us together.

- the hope we need

- the stories we share

- the burdens we unload

- the memories we cherish

- the patience we seek and offer to each other

- and the safety we find here to say what our hearts feel

and to ask what our minds cannot ignore.

Thank you for having the courage to come.

There is strength for healing in this circle

and you are part of that strength."

~From the weekly opening of a grief support group
Used with permission from Janie Cook

Sharing Our Stories Reflection Questions

Introduction (to *Hospice Whispers: Stories of Life*)

1) What words do you think of when you hear the word "hospice?" How has your view of hospice changed in recent years?

_____

_____

_____

_____

2) The word "chaplain" has different connotations for different people. What comes to mind when you think of such professionals? How, in your view, is spiritual care helpful or hurtful to the grief experience?

_____

_____

_____

_____

3) In what ways have you seen grief bring out the best in you and in people you know? In what ways have you seen grief bring out the less-than-life-giving side of you and others?

_____

_____

_____

_____

4) Based on your experience with a loved one's death, what have you learned about what you do and do not want *your* end of life process to be like?

_____

_____

_____

_____

5) How do (or do not) the analogies of labor and giving birth match your experience of the end of life?

_____

_____

_____

_____

6) Describe a time when you have felt someone show up for you in the respectful way described in the "Being a Midwife" quote at the end of the Introduction. Describe a time when you did not experience that. Discuss the differences between how the two experiences felt to you.

_____

_____

_____

_____

ACTION PLAN:

Memories or thoughts arising from this story to hold onto…

Memories or thoughts arising from this story to let go of…

What action steps might I take to encourage my journey of grief further along?

What might I need to take time to simply sit with?

What lessons or insights did I gain through remembering my own or hearing of others' journeys?

Reflect upon the questions above and use the space below to journal your responses:

Why I Do This Work:
Reclaiming Our Connection with Death

1) What was helpful about your experience with caregivers (hospice, hospital, palliative care program, etc.)? What was challenging and/or frustrating?

_____

_____

_____

_____

2) Negative experiences surrounding a loved one's death can complicate the grief experience, re-directing energy and anger toward the frustration or challenge and away from the process of mourning.

Have you found your grief complicated in such a way? If so, discuss those experiences and how you have taken care of yourself, or can take care of yourself, regarding these feelings.

_____

_____

_____

3) If you were a caregiver for your loved one, how adequate do you feel the support you received during their illness and death was?

_____

_____

_____

4) What was your experience with the funeral industry like? What was helpful and what do you wish had been different?

_____

_____

_____

_____

ACTION PLAN:

Memories or thoughts arising from this story to hold onto…

Memories or thoughts arising from this story to let go of…

What action steps might I take to encourage my journey of grief further along?

What might I need to take time to simply sit with?

What lessons or insights did I gain through remembering my own or hearing of others' journeys?

Reflect upon the questions above and use the space below to journal your responses:

_____

_____

_____

_____

_____

_____

_____

_____

_____

_____

What Better Place

1) What have you learned from your experience about what TO say and what NOT to say to someone who is grieving?

_____

_____

_____

_____

2) Describe one or two instances when you have found yourself saying or doing helpful or unhelpful things to and for others when they were grieving?

_____

_____

_____

_____

3) What insight does this give you into what others are thinking and feeling when they stumble in their attempts to support you?

_____

_____

_____

_____

4) How did/do you cope with the less-than-helpful things others have said and done?

_____

_____

_____

5) When someone says or does something that feels hurtful or inappropriate, some feel the need to say so or to set boundaries. Others feel better letting it go. What is your approach? Under what circumstances would *you* choose to or not to respond?

_____

_____

_____

_____

6) If setting boundaries, or naming it out loud when others say something that is not helpful, is what feels best to you, share some examples of what you have said.

_____

_____

_____

_____

7) If/when you feel it is better not to respond, how do you take care of yourself internally to prevent unhelpful comments from harming you?

_____

_____

_____

_____

8) How does it feel when another tries to fix your grief feelings or responses rather than sit with you in them?

_____

_____

_____

9) What do you wish persons would do or say instead of those things you find not helpful?

_____

_____

_____

10) What helps you feel comfortable sitting with others' grief without needing to fix it?

_____

_____

_____

11) What do you think about this sentence from this story, "We can trust love to fill the spaces when we have no words?"

_____

_____

_____

ACTION PLAN:
Memories or thoughts arising from this story to hold onto…
Memories or thoughts arising from this story to let go of…
What action steps might I take to encourage my journey of grief further along?
What might I need to take time to simply sit with?
What lessons or insights did I gain through remembering my own or hearing of others' journeys?

Reflect upon the questions above and use the space below to journal your responses:

_____

_____

_____

_____

_____

_____

_____

_____

_____

_____

_____

_____

_____

_____

_____

_____

Rachmaninoff

1) Dementia can have its own unique grief experience as persons feel a certain sense of abandonment or a series of losses as their loved one declines, loses memory, has personality changes, etc. Have you experienced such a form of grief, with dementia or in other circumstances? What was that like for you?

_____

_____

_____

_____

2) Consider whether there were old, unresolved wounds you experienced with your loved one that made the process of their decline and/or death more challenging. Discuss how these impacted your journey both then and now.

_____

_____

_____

_____

3) Put yourself into this story. Given your experience with the decline and/or death of a loved one, would you have wanted to be told about the moment you missed? Why or why not?

_____

_____

_____

_____

4) How does it feel when someone tells you a story about your loved one that you never heard before, or shares a personal experience they have had with your loved one?

_____

_____

_____

_____

5) Persons' opinions vary about which is harder, the sudden death of a loved one or a slow decline. Each has unique challenges and we try not to compare our pain with others lest it lead us to minimize either our pain or theirs. Discuss your experience and what it was like for you.

_____

_____

_____

_____

6) What do you believe is uniquely difficult about a death due to a slow decline? What is uniquely difficult about a sudden death?

_____

_____

_____

_____

7) Anticipatory grief can show up in many ways, including when we sit over a time with a grief we know is eventually coming, such as when there is a terminal diagnosis. It can also arise when we experience a series of griefs as we watch someone leave us, mentally and/or physically, a little more each day.

If your loved one's death was a slow decline, similar to that of the woman in this story, did you find yourself grieving their death before they died? What was hardest about that for you? Was something of this process helpful to you in some way?

_____

_____

_____

_____

8) Where are you in your relationship to the concept of bittersweet? Are you able to enjoy the sweet or is the bitter still too sharp?

_____

_____

_____

_____

ACTION PLAN:

Memories or thoughts arising from this story to hold onto…

Memories or thoughts arising from this story to let go of…

What action steps might I take to encourage my journey of grief further along?

What might I need to take time to simply sit with?

What lessons or insights did I gain through remembering my own or hearing of others' journeys?

Reflect upon the questions above and use the space below to journal your responses:

_____

_____

_____

_____

_____

_____

A Familiar Tune

1) If your journey involved watching a loved one decline, what was it like for you to see them change day by day? What was the hardest part of this process?

_____

_____

_____

_____

2) What were some of the ways your loved one's personality was still there in the final days or weeks of their life? Were those helpful, challenging, or both? How so?

_____

_____

_____

_____

3) What did/do you want others to know about who your loved one was in his or her healthy, active life? In other words, how would you like for others to remember them?

_____

_____

_____

_____

4) How do you think your loved one would want to be remembered?

_____

_____

_____

_____

ACTION PLAN:

Memories or thoughts arising from this story to hold onto…

Memories or thoughts arising from this story to let go of…

What action steps might I take to encourage my journey of grief further along?

What might I need to take time to simply sit with?

What lessons or insights did I gain through remembering my own or hearing of others' journeys?

Reflect upon the questions above and use the space below to journal your responses:

_____

_____

_____

_____

_____

_____

_____

_____

_____

Let life be as beautiful

as summer flowers

And death as beautiful

as autumn leaves.

~Rabindranath Tagore

Of Course You Feel That Way (Part I)

1) If dementia or some other form of cognitive impairment was part of your loved one's journey, what comes up for you when you read from the first paragraphs of this story, *"It can feel devastating to be seen but not known?"*

_____

_____

_____

_____

2) Even when cognitive impairment isn't part of the journey, roles and relationships still shift naturally as a loved one's illness progresses. Typically strong, capable, independent people increasingly need more help. Outgoing and/or jovial personalities can shift in demeanor.

Patients do not want to feel like a burden to their families and can struggle with the grief of losing independence and control. Those who were the financial providers in a family may no longer be able to provide. Lovers may have little to give.

It can be easy to feel emotionally drained or abandoned or to just miss the person they are not able to be when tired, distracted, and hurting.

Talk or write about what this was like for you. How were you able to still connect with your loved one and where did you feel disconnected? How did you cope with that?

_____

_____

_____

_____

3) If you have experienced loving someone who has dementia, what comes up for you when you read in this story the research that indicates even once a person with dementia forgets a visit, they may still remember the positive emotions that come up as a result of the visit long afterward?

Even if your loved one did not have dementia, often persons reach a stage during illness when they are no longer able to respond as they linger for a period of time in a coma-like state. As discussed elsewhere in *Hospice Whispers* (in "Popcorn and Dominoes"), brain scans at the end of life indicate the last senses to leave us are hearing and smell, meaning we always assume persons can hear us and, on some level, know we are there.

How does this knowledge impact your thoughts and feelings about the visits you were able to make with your loved one?

_____

_____

_____

_____

4) Guilt is a common companion with illness, caregiving, and grief. What was your experience of guilt during your journey? What has helped or worsened that sense of guilt over time? What guilt remains that may still need healing?

_____

_____

_____

_____

5) How does reading the research about the emotional and physical impact, and even mortality risks, that family caregivers may face land inside of you? Does it ring true? Why or why not? How does it impact your view of how we support family caregivers?

_____

_____

_____

_____

6) The idea that hospice staff often encourage family members to visit less, not more, may be surprising for some. What are your reactions to that idea? Is it hard to comprehend? Does it conjure up fear that others will judge you and/or that you will later feel guilty for not doing more?

These ideas can hold loved ones back from taking good care of themselves. After reading this particular chapter, how do you believe we might overcome this barrier to taking good care of ourselves while caring for a loved one who is ill?

_____

_____

_____

_____

7) "…grief is a journey for which there is no shortcut. The only way out is through." What comes up for you when you read this?

_____

_____

_____

_____

8) What do you know of the temptation to want to fix things for those who are hurting and the struggle it can be to sit with pain that cannot be fixed? How do you, or could you, take good care of your own boundaries to allow yourself to be present with pain without needing to make it all better?

_____

_____

_____

_____

9) When others are hurting and you feel empty, how do you respond? What are some helpful coping skills or means of giving yourself a break or escape that may help you take care of yourself during such moments?

_____

_____

_____

_____

_____

10) What have you learned about coping with grief? What new skills have you discovered or acquired?

_____

_____

_____

_____

_____

(Part II—"Big John")

11) The idea that someone who has dementia, some other cognitive impairment, or is otherwise non-responsive could on some level still be there can be hard for some to grasp. What was it like for you when your loved one could not respond as they normally would? How did you cope?

_____

_____

_____

_____

12) Did you want to be there when your loved one died? Did your loved one choose to die alone or with others around? What was that like for you? Are there any lingering regrets about what happened during that time that still need to be processed and relieved in some way? What are you grateful for about that time?

_____

_____

_____

13) Do you feel as if you were able to say a "goodbye" that felt good to you and gave you what you needed? If so, please share that story. If not, share what you wish you could have happen if you could have a do-over. What might you do to give yourself that chance in another way?

_____

_____

_____

ACTION PLAN:

Memories or thoughts arising from this story to hold onto…

Memories or thoughts arising from this story to let go of…

What action steps might I take to encourage my journey of grief further along?

What might I need to take time to simply sit with?

What lessons or insights did I gain through remembering my own or hearing of others' journeys?

Reflect upon the questions above and use the space below to journal your responses:

_____

_____

_____

_____

_____

_____

The deep pain that is felt at the death

of every friendly soul arises

from the feeling that there is

in every individual

something which is inexpressible,

peculiar to him alone,

and is, therefore,

absolutely and irretrievably lost.

~Arthur Schopenhauer

Well I Guess That's Dad

1) What beliefs were you raised with as a child regarding an afterlife? How have your views changed? What of your current views about the afterlife give you peace or comfort and what is challenging for you?

_____

_____

_____

_____

2) What information do you have about your loved one's views of an afterlife, if they believed such existed? What is/was helpful or challenging about their views for you?

_____

_____

_____

_____

3) Were/are children involved in your grief journey with a loved one's illness and/or death? If so, how do you feel that has impacted your own experience of grief?

_____

_____

_____

_____

_____

4) How comfortable are you with the words "death," "dying," etc.?

_____

_____

_____

_____

5) What are some of the euphemisms you have heard used for death with children or even adults? Which feel the worst to you? Are there some that are actually comforting to you?

_____

_____

_____

_____

6) Did you experience your loved one holding on at the end of their life?

_____

_____

_____

_____

7. Do you sense they felt the need to complete some sort of work or goal? What was that like for you?

_____

_____

_____

_____

_____

8) What humorous moments did you experience surrounding the illness and/or death of your loved one?

_____

_____

_____

_____

ACTION PLAN:

Memories or thoughts arising from this story to hold onto…

Memories or thoughts arising from this story to let go of…

What action steps might I take to encourage my journey of grief further along?

What might I need to take time to simply sit with?

What lessons or insights did I gain through remembering my own or hearing of others' journeys?

Reflect upon the questions above and use the space below to journal your responses:

_____

_____

_____

_____

_____

_____

_____

_____

_____

Big Momma

1) What tensions in relationships and between personalities did you experience amongst family and friends surrounding the death of your loved one?

_____

_____

_____

_____

2) How did those tensions impact your process then? How do they impact you now?

_____

_____

_____

_____

3) People express grief in various ways. Some are quiet and tearless while others are loud and cry easily, with everything in between exhibited even in the same family. What is your way of expressing grief? Are there ways that you _wish_ you could grieve (i.e., be more loud and expressive or be less so?) What might it do for your grief process now if you were to allow yourself to try something different?

_____

_____

_____

_____

4) Because each of us grieves differently, tensions may arise when we do not understand another's process, especially when we make assumptions or wrong conclusions about what their way of grieving means. How can we give others room to grieve exactly as they need to without judgment from us?

_____

_____

_____

_____

5) Who was the decision-maker for or head of your family during the death you experienced? How did that help or hurt the process for you?

_____

_____

_____

_____

6) Do you know what it's like to not want to be the grown-up in the room? If so, how do you care for yourself and where do you turn for support in those times?

_____

_____

_____

_____

7) The 84-year-old man, with the 103-year-old mother who had just died, shared, "No matter how old you are, when your parent dies, you feel like you're five years old and all you want is your mommy." Many express feeling orphaned and/or more vulnerable when they become the elder in their family. Some have even said it is easier to ignore the fact that they are going to die someday when there are older relatives "ahead of them in line" to die.

Does the illusion of a buffer between us and death help us ignore the reality that ours will come someday? When our parents, aunts and uncles, and older siblings die, it can leave us more starkly aware that we could be next.

What has your experience been with this dynamic? How has it impacted your grief journey? How does it impact your role in your family? How does it influence the way you live your life?

_____

_____

_____

_____

8) Where do you feel you have the most room to grieve freely, exactly as you need, without judgment?

_____

_____

_____

_____

ACTION PLAN:

Memories or thoughts arising from this story to hold onto…

Memories or thoughts arising from this story to let go of…

What action steps might I take to encourage my journey of grief further along?

What might I need to take time to simply sit with?

What lessons or insights did I gain through remembering my own or hearing of others' journeys?

Reflect upon the questions above and use the space below to journal your responses:

So, this is what my being broken sounded like . . .

"crying on the outside, screaming on the inside

stumbling & grasping

searching and trying to focus"

"my days feel like burdens"

"a piece of my heart is gone

something central to my breathing is missing

I can't figure out how to be me"

"Tears are my only words."

"The world feels blank in places — empty of the beauty you radiated

jagged, torn, ragged . . . familiar but with holes in it

I'm singed, seared, burned around the edges of my life."

"I'm gasping for spiritual breath."

It seems fair to say that being broken is something that happens outside our control, shattering life as we know it. Loss obliterates gift and is an honest, full body response to being at the mercy of indescribable sadness.

Then, this is what my being broken open sounds like . . .

"who's to say how long a life should be—

it was long enough to love deeply and that is no small legacy"

"this has pushed all the negative emotions out of me . . . and left me with only love and tenderness"

"I will miss him every day of my life

it is that simple and that strong

his life – either here or there—is woven into and through mine"

"living wide open seems the only way now

> *without protection or fear*

> *being vulnerable as honest as I can be*

> *but kind"*

"I want to live with the door of my heart open . . .

let this make me soft and strong all at once"

Being broken open, is something we allow to happen. It feels all the devastation but doesn't turn away . . . and as it feels, it drops small seeds of healing into the shattered heart. What was surprising to me was that both seem to happen simultaneously—at first in an uneven jerky movement with no rhythm or predictability. But in time, as healing takes hold, the unevenness smoothes out and life begins to flow again—having learned to absorb this part of truth into our being.

-Janie Cook

The Day of the Dying

1) If you are aware, where did your loved one want to die? Was that medically and/or financially feasible for their particular case? How do you feel the experience would have been different had they died elsewhere?

_____

_____

_____

_____

2) What came up for you when Bernadette shared about her mom? Specifically when she said she, "...was beating herself up, saying she should have said more, should have done this or that. But when she went back to this story I wrote again and again she realized it was all absolutely perfect!"

In the Introduction to this workbook (pg. 11), I mentioned this story specifically and the importance of sharing our experiences to help us gain clarity. How has journaling and/or sharing your stories helped you find more peace with your own experience?

_____

_____

_____

_____

3) Bernadette shared that her brother asked her if she, "didn't feel burdened having to stay?" She replied that she did not, "in fact I felt gifted." Different people have different comfort levels with the tasks involved in caring for a loved one.

What felt like a burden to you? What felt like a gift, or what have you since come to see as a gift? How well were you and other loved ones able to accept what one another could and could not handle doing in terms of being present during the final weeks and days of illness?

_____

_____

_____

_____

4) Bernadette writes of her father's silence lengthening a few days before the very end after, "he had said what he wanted to say and so had we…"
Some persons who are dying go into this silence before those around them feel that everything has been said. This can be hard for loved ones who often question if the person is angry with them. It can lead to hurt feelings and misunderstandings.

Many end of life professionals believe this is not a withdrawal of love, but is simply about the person's need to focus inward to process what is happening. Dying is a new experience and they may have a need to psychologically prepare.

Did you experience this drawing inward by your loved one? If so, what was that like for you then? How do you understand it and feel about it now?

_____

_____

_____

_____

5) When Bernadette writes about helping her father with the condom catheter, she says, "…all of us (were) aware of a lifetime of modesty wiped out with one terminal illness." Where did the dynamic of modesty come up in your situation? How did you handle it? Do you still experience any emotional wounds from this?

_____

_____

_____

_____

6) Our personalities may shift with the distraction and fatigue of being ill or facing death and grief, but they do not go away. Humor may remain, as we read with Bernadette's father making the joke about not wanting to get his wife pregnant and then leave her. What role did and does humor play in your circumstance? How else may it help you now?

_____

_____

_____

_____

7) In this story, we see another glimpse of the role reversal that can occur during caregiving, such as Bernadette lifting her father up higher in his bed. Where did you see roles reverse with your loved ones? What was that like for you?

_____

_____

_____

_____

8) Consider this quote from the story: "The little kids were there too, earnestly in and out of the room with their play and myriad cousins. Occasionally, they'd forget death was at hand, only to solemnly remember."

Children tend to handle grief in just this way, moving in and out of it as they are able to handle it emotionally and process it cognitively, depending on where they are developmentally. (This also means that grief may be re-processed by children as they age and deepen in their ability to comprehend and feel the impact of a death).

What was your experience of children in the death of your loved one? What was it like to see their reactions to the process?

_____

_____

_____

9) In many ways, children are good role models for us as we, too, need breaks from grieving every now and then—to give our hearts and minds room to rest and catch up in processing what's happening. Where were and are you able to give yourself room to ebb and flow into and out of grief?

_____

_____

_____

_____

10) In portraying the children coming in and out as grandpa lay dying, Bernadette writes that they marveled "…at the fact that all these adults they knew and loved were all crying together. And when they caught our eye, our faces lifted through our tears and they marveled again that we could smile while we wept."

Where have you experienced being able to smile while weeping? What does it mean to be able to do that? What is your relationship with tears? Are they welcome, or is it hard for you to let yourself express them?

_____

_____

_____

_____

11) Bernadette expressed gratitude for an uncle who told them, "…not to panic at death but rather, to linger in the passing." Have you experienced such gentle space around death? If not, what would you like for yourself and your loved ones in the future?

_____

_____

_____

_____

12) This is another view of the funeral home personnel being caring and sensitive to the needs of the family. What thoughts come up for you about this now regarding your own experience with the funeral industry?

_____

_____

_____

_____

13) This story closes with the following lines, "They lifted him ever so gently and walked out to the hearse followed by the five-year-old who perhaps never again would think of death as scary. The obituary read: Dean Charles Noll passed away at home on August 3, 2003. His death was gentle. He is survived by the stories we tell."

The primary goal of *Hospice Whispers: Stories of Life* was to make death seem a little less scary and to help persons understand hospice better and fear it less. How has your own circumstance influenced how you see death, for better or worse? How have the stories you've read and heard from others impacted you and your feelings about death, for better or worse?

_____

_____

_____

_____

14) You may have witnessed your loved one have a death that was NOT gentle, with terminal restlessness or pain or other symptoms. What was that like for you? Have you recovered from any trauma this may have caused you, or is there still healing left for you to do in this area?

_____

_____

_____

_____

15) One of the hardest things for some adults is the knowledge that future generations will know the person who is dying only from stories. What stories do you most want future generations to know about the person you love who has died?

_____

_____

_____

_____

16) What can this teach us about our own stories that we want to pass down and leave behind when we die?

_____

_____

_____

_____

ACTION PLAN:

Memories or thoughts arising from this story to hold onto…

Memories or thoughts arising from this story to let go of…

What action steps might I take to encourage my journey of grief further along?

What might I need to take time to simply sit with?

What lessons or insights did I gain through remembering my own or hearing of others' journeys?

Reflect upon the questions above and use the space below to journal your responses:

_____

_____

_____

_____

_____

There is a sacredness in tears.

They are not the mark of weakness,

but of power.

They speak more eloquently

than ten thousand tongues.

They are the messengers

of overwhelming grief,

of deep contrition,

and of unspeakable love.

~Attributed to Washington Irving

Your Mom is so Sweet

1) How did your relationship with your loved one differ from the relationship others had with them? What was it like for you to grieve alongside others who had a different experience of that person? For instance, if you were close to the deceased and others had hard feelings to express that you did not experience, or vice versa, what was it like for you?

_____

_____

_____

2) Did your loved one's personality change in the process of illness or aging? What was challenging about those changes? How were those changes helpful, if at all? For instance, did a grouchier personality become more mellow as the person aged or as their illness progressed?

_____

_____

_____

3) Some feel guilty about feeling relief when a family member dies, whether that is the sum of their feelings or only one small part of their reaction. What was your experience of relief after a death? Where and how were you able to express the full range of your feelings?

_____

_____

_____

_____

4) If you went through hospice or another healthcare organization, what was your experience of volunteers?

_____

_____

_____

_____

5) How was your loved one's public face different from the private face that you saw when others were not around? What was that like for you?

_____

_____

_____

_____

6) How did/do you hold that space between being honest about your experience of a person with the desire to not tear someone down publicly?

_____

_____

_____

_____

7) Disenfranchised grief is that which is not known, acknowledged, or understood by society. When this occurs others do not know to offer support (i.e., when a secret relationship ends) or they do not offer adequate support out of a lack of understanding (i.e., after a miscarriage, death of a pet, or any time others begin to feel that someone should be over their grief within a certain period of time).

When a deceased loved one was challenging or even abusive to live with, most others around us will not know the private story. As a result, those who have been victimized may be reminded painfully of the original trauma, and the secrets that surrounded it, as others praise the one who perpetrated the abuse as a wonderful person, not knowing the damage he or she also caused.

Others may not realize the extra triggers and confusion that can occur when a person with whom we had a challenging relationship dies. As a result, they may not offer us adequate support.

What, if any, has been your experience of disenfranchised grief? What healing might you still be in need of that you could receive from others about this now?

_____

_____

_____

8) How would you answer the two questions in this story about A) what you miss the most and B) what you do not miss about your loved one?

_____

_____

_____

9) What was it like for you to hear the words said about your loved one at services after their death? What things were said by the officiant that felt helpful or harmful?

_____

_____

_____

10) Are compassion and forgiveness a part of your story at this point? How is where you are now helpful for you at this moment? Where would you like to be in three months? Six months? A year? What do you think it would take for you to find your way to a place that feels better?

_____

_____

_____

11) Again I ask, what things left unsaid or undone might you still want to address in some way to the one who has died? How can others support you with that process?

_____

_____

_____

_____

ACTION PLAN:

Memories or thoughts arising from this story to hold onto…

Memories or thoughts arising from this story to let go of…

What action steps might I take to encourage my journey of grief further along?

What might I need to take time to simply sit with?

What lessons or insights did I gain through remembering my own or hearing of others' journeys?

Reflect upon the questions above and use the space below to journal your responses:

_____

_____

_____

_____

_____

_____

_____

_____

_____

_____

Contemplation

1) What were some of the frustrations you faced with your loved one as he or she went through the process they needed to go through in their illness or decline?

_____

_____

_____

_____

2) One question we often ask ourselves as professional caregivers is, "Is this mine to do?" If we do for others what they can do for themselves, we do too much. This can be disrespectful of them and over-burdening for us. In what ways did you find yourself walking the line between doing things for someone versus giving them room to have their own process?

_____

_____

_____

_____

3) What was your own process of preparing for your loved one's decline or death like?

_____

_____

_____

_____

4) Where did you see issues of control in the process you experienced or are currently experiencing?

_____

_____

_____

_____

5) Have you experienced the freedom of letting go of power struggles? What was that like and how did you get there?

_____

_____

_____

_____

6) How did you handle your fears that others would think poorly of you because of something your loved one did or did not decide to do in the midst of their decline?

_____

_____

_____

_____

ACTION PLAN:

Memories or thoughts arising from this story to hold onto…

Memories or thoughts arising from this story to let go of…

What action steps might I take to encourage my journey of grief further along?

What might I need to take time to simply sit with?

What lessons or insights did I gain through remembering my own or hearing of others' journeys?

Reflect upon the questions above and use the space below to journal your responses:

_____

_____

_____

_____

_____

_____

_____

_____

_____

_____

_____

_____

_____

_____

_____

_____

_____

There's a Sweet Spirit

1) Did your loved one experience a rally or one last burst of energy and alertness often described as happening at the end of life? Whatever your answer, what was that like for you?

_____

_____

_____

_____

2) Many describe moments in which they feel their loved one came to give them some sort of message in some way. Where or how have you felt or sensed your loved one with you, if at all, since their dying?

_____

_____

_____

_____

3) What are your views about how our loved ones do or do not watch over or speak to us after they died? How do these views help and/or hinder your process?

_____

_____

_____

_____

_____

4) Those who believe in a deity (G-d, or other names may be used, depending on your religion or beliefs) may have been taught not to question what happens after death, while others are encouraged to do so. Many struggle with existential questions (Why do bad things happen to good people; why does suffering happen; where is a good and loving G-d when it hurts, etc.). Some feel it is safe and appropriate to grapple with these questions and others do not feel comfortable doing so. Discuss your relationship with asking such questions.

_____

_____

_____

_____

5) Consider the following quote from this story: "But day after day, things beyond my ability to explain or comprehend happen around us in this work that humble me, give me pause, and assure me that something greater than me is working in this world. I know I can trust it to hold us all and help us find our way, if only we can listen and let it be present with us."

Does this passage resonate in any way with your experience of the death of your loved one? If so, how?

_____

_____

_____

_____

ACTION PLAN:
Memories or thoughts arising from this story to hold onto...
Memories or thoughts arising from this story to let go of...
What action steps might I take to encourage my journey of grief further along?
What might I need to take time to simply sit with?
What lessons or insights did I gain through remembering my own or hearing of others' journeys?

Reflect upon the questions above and use the space below to journal your responses:

Little Boy Lost

1) What is your relationship with mystery, or things for which there seem to be no answers available at this time?

_____

_____

_____

_____

2) Did your loved one express fear or anger or other emotions during their dying process? If so, what was it like for you to be around those feelings and not be able to fix them?

_____

_____

_____

_____

3) What do you think about the man's description of himself as a child who felt lost? Have you felt like this since your loved one died? What gives you reassurance that you are on the right path toward healing for yourself?

_____

_____

_____

_____

4) What do you do with the questions that have no definite answers? How important is it to the healing of grief to find answers? If healing does not lie in finding answers for you, what do you believe healing depends upon?

_____

_____

_____

_____

ACTION PLAN:

Memories or thoughts arising from this story to hold onto…

Memories or thoughts arising from this story to let go of…

What action steps might I take to encourage my journey of grief further along?

What might I need to take time to simply sit with?

What lessons or insights did I gain through remembering my own or hearing of others' journeys?

Reflect upon the questions above and use the space below to journal your responses:

_____

_____

_____

_____

_____

_____

_____

_____

_____

Wounds of the spirit…are most gently soothed and made whole by the passing years. Under the old scars flows again the calm, healthful tide of life…Under a great loss the heart impetuously cries that it can never be happy again, and perhaps in its desperation says that it wishes never to be comforted. But though angels do not fly down to open the grave and restore the lost, the days and months come as angels with healing in their wings. Under their touch aching regret passes into tender memory; into hands that were empty new joys are softly pressed; and the heart that was like the trees stripped of its leaves and beaten by winter's tempests is clothed again with the green of spring.

~George S. Merriam

Moaning to Singing

1) Have you ever felt abandoned by G-d , your loved ones, or your friends? How does that feeling impact you now?

_____

_____

_____

_____

2) When you read that I did not want to "rob her of the dignity of finding her own answers," did that idea ring true for you? How do you understand dignity and the role of letting others find their own answers?

_____

_____

_____

_____

3) I once heard that we have permission to ask our questions as long as we need to ask them. Does that sound comforting to you? Why or why not?

_____

_____

_____

_____

4) Trying to put a bandage on another's pain is a strong temptation for most of us. After your experience with grief, what would you say to others about the benefit of just sitting with someone in their pain?

_____

_____

_____

5) Describe a time when someone was able to sit with your pain and not try to fix it, but rather just be with you in that uncomfortable place. What kind of a gift did they give you by doing so?

_____

_____

_____

_____

6) How well are you able to sit with your own pain without fixing it? What is difficult about doing so? What helps you do that?

_____

_____

_____

7) In the practice of sitting Shiva in the Jewish tradition, persons are instructed to sit with the grieving family and to follow their lead one hundred percent. If they want to talk about the weather or sports or a television show, you join them there. If they want to speak of their loved one, you go there with them and do not try to turn the conversation in a direction that is more comfortable for you. How do you think all of us could benefit from such a method of presence with grief?

_____

_____

_____

ACTION PLAN:

Memories or thoughts arising from this story to hold onto…

Memories or thoughts arising from this story to let go of…

What action steps might I take to encourage my journey of grief further along?

What might I need to take time to simply sit with?

What lessons or insights did I gain through remembering my own or hearing of others' journeys?

Reflect upon the questions above and use the space below to journal your responses:

_____

_____

_____

_____

_____

_____

_____

_____

_____

_____

_____

_____

_____

_____

_____

The Shaman

1) Many persons experience anger with religion, especially after suffering some loss or tragedy. Is this something you have felt? If so, have you had a safe space to voice your feelings and struggles? If not, where might that safe space be?

_____

_____

_____

_____

2) What has been your experience with ritual? It does not necessarily need to be religious in nature; saying "hello" and "goodbye" are rituals that mark times of transition. How might familiar, or even brand new, rituals help you during this time of grief and life transition?

_____

_____

_____

_____

3) What do you think helped the man in the story the most?

_____

_____

_____

_____

4) What assumptions might some chaplains or other clergy make that might get in the way of the freedom this man found?

_____

_____

_____

_____

5) When he said, "It's like it's all okay now, in some way," what do you think he meant?

_____

_____

_____

_____

6) Can you imagine saying that to yourself about the death of your loved one—that's it's okay in some way? What do you feel when you think about saying that?

_____

_____

_____

_____

ACTION PLAN:

Memories or thoughts arising from this story to hold onto…

Memories or thoughts arising from this story to let go of…

What action steps might I take to encourage my journey of grief further along?

What might I need to take time to simply sit with?

What lessons or insights did I gain through remembering my own or hearing of others' journeys?

Reflect upon the questions above and use the space below to journal your responses:

Ritual

1) What is one thing about your loved one that others did not quite understand or may have misunderstood?

_____

_____

_____

_____

2) Was your loved one open with their feelings or more closed? What was this like for you in your relationship, especially toward the end of their life?

_____

_____

_____

_____

_____

3) What was a simple or guilty pleasure your loved one had?

_____

_____

_____

_____

_____

4) In this story, the teacher qualities came out in this patient even toward the end of her life. What qualities of your loved one still existed in their later days?

_____

_____

_____

_____

5) What lessons did you learn from your loved one's process (lengthy illness, sudden accident, etc.), meaning, in what way were they a teacher during this time?

_____

_____

_____

_____

6) How do you think ritual was helpful for this woman? How is it helpful for you?

_____

_____

_____

_____

7) In what ways was her idea of ritual similar to or different from yours?

_____

_____

_____

_____

8) What is ritualized in your life that brings you comfort? Are there any rituals you find empty of meaning?

_____

_____

_____

_____

9) Was there a ritual of some sort following the death of your loved one (funeral, memorial, wake, etc)? What was or was not comforting about it? What would have made it even more helpful for your grieving process?

_____

_____

_____

_____

ACTION PLAN:

Memories or thoughts arising from this story to hold onto…

Memories or thoughts arising from this story to let go of…

What action steps might I take to encourage my journey of grief further along?

What might I need to take time to simply sit with?

What lessons or insights did I gain through remembering my own or hearing of others' journeys?

Reflect upon the questions above and use the space below to journal your responses:

_____

_____

_____

_____

_____

_____

When I Heard the Learn'd Astronomer

When I heard the learn'd astronomer,

When the proofs, the figures,

were ranged in columns before me,

When I was shown the charts and the diagrams, to add, divide, and

measure them,

When I sitting heard the astronomers where he lectured with much

applause in the lecture-room,

How soon unaccountable

I became tired and sick,

Till rising and gliding out

I wander'd off by myself,

In the mystical moist night-air,

and from time to time,

Look'd up in perfect silence at the stars.

~Walt Whitman

Assuming Mary

1) What were some of the missteps others made during your time of grief?

_____

_____

_____

_____

2) How well were you able to repair and recover from those?

_____

_____

_____

_____

3) What do you want others to know about your loved one? What false assumptions are you afraid they might make about them?

_____

_____

_____

_____

4) Do you ever sense that others make inaccurate assumptions about you? What do you suspect they assume? What would you want them to know about the grief you are going through?

_____

_____

_____

_____

ACTION PLAN:

Memories or thoughts arising from this story to hold onto…

Memories or thoughts arising from this story to let go of…

What action steps might I take to encourage my journey of grief further along?

What might I need to take time to simply sit with?

What lessons or insights did I gain through remembering my own or hearing of others' journeys?

Reflect upon the questions above and use the space below to journal your responses:

_____

_____

_____

_____

_____

_____

_____

_____

Asking the Questions

1) What particular customs or beliefs that you and/or your family hold came into play during your loved one's death? How well did others respect your practices?

_____

_____

_____

_____

2) In what ways did you feel healthcare staff and/or friends missed seeing your needs during the time of your loved one's death?

_____

_____

_____

_____

_____

3) What has the experience of your loved one's death specifically taught you about what you hope for yourself when you are dying? What do you want YOUR end of life to look like?

_____

_____

_____

_____

4) What, if anything, would you change about the death of your loved one? What do you wish you could do differently?

_____

_____

_____

_____

ACTION PLAN:

Memories or thoughts arising from this story to hold onto…

Memories or thoughts arising from this story to let go of…

What action steps might I take to encourage my journey of grief further along?

What might I need to take time to simply sit with?

What lessons or insights did I gain through remembering my own or hearing of others' journeys?

Reflect upon the questions above and use the space below to journal your responses:

_____

_____

_____

_____

_____

_____

_____

_____

Redemption

1) Have you ever felt you were being punished by a deity? What was that like for you? How, if at all, have your views changed since that time?

\
\
\
\
\

2) Have you ever felt affirmed and supported by a deity? What was that like for you?

\
\
\
\

3) What spiritual questions have come up for you since your loved one died? Which ones might you still wrestle with?

\
\
\
\

4) How are your beliefs the same and/or different from what they were before your grief began? How does it feel for your beliefs to change?

_____

_____

_____

_____

5) Have you encountered anyone who wanted to give you spiritual answers? How does that feel? How do you respond?

_____

_____

_____

_____

ACTION PLAN:

Memories or thoughts arising from this story to hold onto…

Memories or thoughts arising from this story to let go of…

What action steps might I take to encourage my journey of grief further along?

What might I need to take time to simply sit with?

What lessons or insights did I gain through remembering my own or hearing of others' journeys?

**Reflect upon the questions above and use the space below to journal your responses:**

_____

_____

_____

_____

_____

Sit with Me First

1) Was there someone in particular in healthcare or otherwise related to your loved one's death who gained your deep trust in some way? If so, how did they manage to do so? What did it mean for you to have that experience?

_____

_____

_____

_____

2) Sometimes the most comforting comments come from the people we least expect to offer them. Share about a time when someone surprised you with a comment that helped you get through a difficult moment.

_____

_____

_____

_____

3) Knowing what a loved one wants with regards to end of life medical care, such as artificial hydration, nutrition, feeding, breathing, etc. can make it easier on families because it alleviates them of having to make heartbreaking decisions at an already painful time. What was your experience with these decisions if your loved one faced an illness or injury? What do you wish had been different about that process?

_____

_____

_____

_____

ACTION PLAN:

Memories or thoughts arising from this story to hold onto…

Memories or thoughts arising from this story to let go of…

What action steps might I take to encourage my journey of grief further along?

What might I need to take time to simply sit with?

What lessons or insights did I gain through remembering my own or hearing of others' journeys?

Reflect upon the questions above and use the space below to journal your responses:

_____

_____

_____

_____

_____

_____

_____

_____

_____

_____

_____

_____

_____

I'm Trying to Die Here

1) Where did you or your loved ones find humor in the midst of your sadness or grief? What was that like for you? For them? Is it helpful or disturbing for you?

_____

_____

_____

_____

2) When and why might humor not feel good to someone who is hurting?

_____

_____

_____

_____

3) What is your reaction to my shock at the dark humor of the therapy team I worked with in my younger years, as described in the beginning of the story?

_____

_____

_____

4) Where do you believe the line is between irreverence and humor? Does that line change for you at times?

_____

_____

_____

_____

5) I mentioned in this story that most often we healthcare staff get to answer the same questions multiple times. When we experience grief, our thoughts and feelings can be quite disorganized as much of our inner physical and emotional resources are going toward coping with the stress. What types of forgetfulness or fuzzy-headedness did/ do you experience? How do you find gentleness for yourself during these times?

_____

_____

_____

_____

6) What differences are/were there between the ways you and other family members grieved and dealt with the stress of facing the death of a loved one? How do/did you navigate those different ways of grieving and handling stress?

_____

_____

_____

_____

ACTION PLAN:
Memories or thoughts arising from this story to hold onto…
Memories or thoughts arising from this story to let go of…
What action steps might I take to encourage my journey of grief further along?
What might I need to take time to simply sit with?
What lessons or insights did I gain through remembering my own or hearing of others' journeys?

Reflect upon the questions above and use the space below to journal your responses:

Anarchy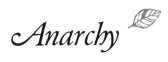

1) Until we have another tool in our tool belt that we feel comfortable using to help us cope with grief, we will continue to wield our denial like a shield. Denial acts as natural, helpful, and even adaptive and healthy emotional shock absorbers. They help us to process through what's happening slowly, as we are able to handle it.

However, the term "denial" is often seen as something pejorative; as if those experiencing it are weak, unhealthy, immature, or just flat out resistant. Where do you think our judgment of denial comes from? How can we get past those judgments to accept denial as the appropriate, and often necessary, part of grief that it truly is?

_____

_____

_____

2) Dr. Monica Williams-Murphy writes: "Failure to disclose the truth at the end of life is moral medical malpractice." (oktodie.com) What do you think about this quote? How did a doctor or other medical professionals' willingness, or lack thereof, to discuss end of life issues such as hospice help or hurt your journey?

_____

_____

_____

3) What surprised you about those who came close (friends, faith community, colleagues, neighbors, etc.) vs. those who appeared to not be around during your loved one's illness and death? How did you interpret their presence, or the lack thereof?

_____

_____

_____

4) It can be easy to take things personally and feel angry and abandoned if others are not around as much as we would like when we are struggling or suffering. What do you believe helped the woman in this story not hold a grudge against her absent faith community?

_____

_____

_____

_____

_____

5) Fear of going to sleep is a common struggle that those living their final days may face. If this was part of your experience, what did you attempt or find actually helped your loved one to feel safe?

_____

_____

_____

_____

_____

6) Family struggles are a fact of life. Just because we are facing death does not mean that old arguments, personality differences, wounds, etc. just go away. How did you notice you and your family handling such issues? For instance, did you talk about the issues or simply find some sort of fragile peace? Did you find a way to truly let go, breathe deeply, and choose to walk away from conflict or did you feel it important to confront it head on? How well did your chosen course of action, or inaction, work? How present are those dynamics in your family now? Have they changed for better or worse?

_____

_____

_____

_____

7) According to various theoretical models, we are quietly assigned roles to play in families and groups. The idea of a scapegoat or black sheep of the family is not a new concept in life or literature. Whom do you consider to be the person designated by your family to be the black sheep? How did that dynamic come up during or influence what you experienced around the time of your loved one's death? Has a resolution or healing occurred around this? Where does the need for healing remain?

_____

_____

_____

8) Did you find yourself having or facing others' judgments about the way your loved one and/or family handled your environment (noise, lighting, topics of conversation), or anything else, as your loved one died? How did you handle that scrutiny? Are there ways that your own judgments, or others', are still a struggle for you? What might you do to free yourself from these?

_____

_____

_____

ACTION PLAN:

Memories or thoughts arising from this story to hold onto…

Memories or thoughts arising from this story to let go of…

What action steps might I take to encourage my journey of grief further along?

What might I need to take time to simply sit with?

What lessons or insights did I gain through remembering my own or hearing of others' journeys?

Reflect upon the questions above and use the space below to journal your responses:

_____

_____

_____

_____

_____

Sometimes grief seems like too much to bear

and we instinctively hide seeking some way to dull its impact.

And that is exactly the moment we are invited

to soften enough,

to open enough,

to have courage enough

to see that Now is more

than the complexity of grief descending upon us.

Each grieving moment is layered with

the vast void of loss, that is true but also,

the "nows" past when our hearts

were light with joy and limitless with hope.

Now is complex,

an intricately woven truth

made of memory, emptiness, gratitude and loss,

weaving the tapestry of a whole heart.

And peace is the One Thread

That binds and embraces it all

infusing us with a strength that is surprising.

~Janie Cook

Popcorn and Dominoes

1) What do you think and/or feel when you read the following quote that begins this story? "We really don't know how to do this 'death' thing much anymore. More accurately, we don't think we know how to do it because we've forgotten that this is simply part of life and we really can't 'do it wrong.' We've forgotten that we know how to do this."

_____

_____

_____

_____

2) How well do you feel you were able to say and do everything that needed to be said and done with your loved one before their death? If there were things done or not done that you regret, how might you offload those now?

Some write letters then burn or bury them, have a friend or therapist listen as if they are the deceased loved one and say all that needs to be said, or draw what they would have liked. Sometimes, naming regrets is all that is needed. Some find that a creative ritual or even professional suggestions allow them to find a place of peace, which is important. Whatever is right for you, and whenever it seems right for you to do it, trust yourself to find it.

_____

_____

_____

_____

3) Caregivers are said to be the silent victims in medical situations. What did you feel was your role in caring for your loved one? Were you a hands-on caregiver or were you the behind the scenes support like the one who ran errands? Did you build a wheelchair ramp or tell your loved one jokes? Did you love and send thoughts or prayers from afar or handle insurance paperwork and phone calls or simply sit with them and offer your presence or be a social support for other loved ones?

Whatever you did, how did it feel to be in that role? Was it helpful to you to give care or did you feel put-upon, helpless, useless, left out, resentful, resented…? What was it like to be you during your loved one's illness and decline? What areas might still need resolution or healing regarding these dynamics?

_____

_____

_____

_____

4) An important aspect of resilience, or our ability to recover from difficulties, is the ability to regularly practice gratitude. What is on your gratitude list for your loved ones and others' actions and support during the death of your loved one and your resulting grief?

_____

_____

_____

_____

5) What sounds and smells appeared to be comforting to your loved one? When the time of your death comes, what smells and sounds would be comforting for you to experience?

_____

_____

_____

_____

6) Many want to be present at the exact moment their loved one dies, and often feel shame (about others' judgments) or guilt (from their own judgments) if they are not there. However, we caution that if a person wants to die alone, they will, even if their loved ones sit vigil 24/7 at the bedside. They will wait. Others wait for people to be present before they die. What was your experience? Were you relieved or bothered by how the events unfolded in your case?

_____

_____

_____

_____

7) Who, if anyone, do you want present with you when you die?

_____

_____

_____

_____

ACTION PLAN:

Memories or thoughts arising from this story to hold onto…

Memories or thoughts arising from this story to let go of…

What action steps might I take to encourage my journey of grief further along?

What might I need to take time to simply sit with?

What lessons or insights did I gain through remembering my own or hearing of others' journeys?

Reflect upon the questions above and use the space below to journal your responses:

_____

_____

_____

_____

_____

_____

May you notice the beauty that is around you today . . .

may you pause in whatever busy-ness to take it in . . .

and may it soak into the torn places of your heart

and bring comfort. . .

~Janie Cook

Unexpected Gifts

1) What has been your experience with the death of a child or teen?

_____

_____

_____

_____

2) We don't *compare* grief, lest a person minimize their own pain if they believe it to be somehow less challenging than another's experience. For example, some may say, "Oh, they've had it much worse than I have."

This can lead a person to not feel as if they have a right to grieve as deeply or as long as they may need to. It can also leave them feeling guilty or ashamed about how they feel. This downplaying of our circumstance can be a defense mechanism our mind uses to try to avoid pain.

How have you seen your own natural defenses attempt to minimize your pain?

_____

_____

_____

_____

3) While we do not compare, there are forms of grief that have unique characteristics that challenge us in different ways, such as grief related to a trauma or a sudden death. The death of a child or other young person can pose such a challenge for us. What are some of the unique issues that arise when a child dies? How do you make sense of or come to terms with the death of a child?

(**SPECIAL NOTE:** If processing this question with others, please remember to not tell someone who has experienced the death of their child, or a child close to them, how they should think, feel, or believe about their story.

This may leave them feeling angry, isolated, judged, or shamed; which only worsens the experience of grief. There are no right or wrong answers here, just the things that help us find meaning, peace, and comfort; which will likely differ from person to person).

_____

_____

_____

_____

4) It is natural for humans to think that parents will not outlive their children. When it does occur, it poses an existential challenge—something that flies in the face of how we believe the world should be, how we make sense of things, and how we understand questions of existence and meaning and suffering. We may hear, or find ourselves saying, "Parents should never have to bury a child," or "Children should be able to grow up and live out their whole lives."

Similar existential challenges include, "Good people shouldn't suffer," and "Life should not be so unfair." What beliefs of your own have been challenged during your journey of grief? How has grappling with those questions supported or hindered your process?

_____

_____

_____

_____

5) Grieving parents often state their child's life cannot be measured in hours, days, or years, but by the love their presence generated in the world—however long they were physically with us. How do you describe and find meaning, not in the death of a child, but in the value of their life?

_____

_____

_____

_____

6) The topic of clichés comes up in other stories in this book. What are some of the other clichés you have heard about the death of a child? What other thoughts do you have about how clichés may make a person's grief harder to bear?

_____

_____

_____

_____

7) What have you seen of kids' resilience around and acceptance of death?

_____

_____

_____

_____

8) Bradie had her own view of the afterlife. In other stories, the idea of an afterlife has been raised. It bears asking again, how does your view help (or hurt) you as you walk through grief?

_____

_____

_____

_____

9) Rodney shares that this experience helped him learn how important it is "to listen for, and learn" what it is that persons want and need from us as they face their final days and simply be present in whatever ways they need.

A woman recently wrote me an email thanking me for the way the *Hospice Whispers* book helped her give her mother the exact end of life experience her mother wanted and needed by putting her own ideas and judgments aside. She said it wound up being a beautiful gift for her mother and for herself.

In what ways were you able to give this experience of a death on your loved one's own terms, and in their own way? If there were/are ways that were/are not possible, how have you, or might you, come to terms with and accept that things may not go as you would like?

_____

_____

_____

_____

10) What unexpected gifts did you find yourself receiving from your loved one as they went through the process of dying?

_____

_____

_____

ACTION PLAN:

Memories or thoughts arising from this story to hold onto…

Memories or thoughts arising from this story to let go of…

What action steps might I take to encourage my journey of grief further along?

What might I need to take time to simply sit with?

What lessons or insights did I gain through remembering my own or hearing of others' journeys?

Reflect upon the questions above and use the space below to journal your responses:

_____

_____

_____

_____

_____

_____

_____

First you try to take in all that is lost . . .

the dreams that will never be,

the deafening absence,

the precious reminders of the presence of this child

that literally rip a hole in your heart each time you see them

and, at the same time, you try to take in all the amazing gratitude you feel . . . ,

for the unforgettable moments you have been given,

for the vivid memories that replay like a beloved movie in your mind, and

for the amazing gift of a love as immense as this ?

Grief is so confusing! It is packed with both of these heavy opposites. So, we careen from one to the other like a marble in a pinball machine – bouncing first one way then another. It is enough to make you crazy! It does make you crazy.

I carry an image in my mind of what healing looks like. It is standing with both feet planted firmly on the earth, arms outstretched, palms up . . . holding the son I have lost in one hand and the son I have been so graciously given to love in the other. In my better moments, I am balanced between these two truths. And, I believe that healing is learning to keep this balance until it becomes so familiar to us that we do it without thinking. . . . gently holding one reality and then the other . . . . accepting the truth of both.

~Janie Cook

The Gifts We Cannot Refuse

1) The woman in this story spoke of a moment in her childhood when she became clear that G-d was with her and that assurance helped her to never feel afraid or alone, again. Fear of being alone, of feeling abandoned, can be a challenge for both those who are facing the end of life and those who are facing the loss of someone they love.

What helps you cope with any feelings of fear or abandonment that you have experienced in the midst of your grief?

_____

_____

_____

_____

2) Consider the quote from this story: "But we look for ways to hold space for all of this without carrying it with us. If we can find that balance, then it is a joy."

We often speak of creating a container for our grief, a moment or special time of day that we set aside in the midst of our busy lives to focus on the mixture of feelings we carry. When work and family responsibilities must be done, how do you hold at least some space for your grief?

_____

_____

_____

_____

_____

3) What comes to your mind when you hear that quote above about "holding space for all of this without carrying it with us?" What sort of balance do you believe I'm talking about? What does it look like for you?

_____

_____

_____

_____

4) Is joy even a part of your vocabulary yet in relation to your grief? If so, what does it look like for you?

_____

_____

_____

_____

ACTION PLAN:

Memories or thoughts arising from this story to hold onto…

Memories or thoughts arising from this story to let go of…

What action steps might I take to encourage my journey of grief further along?

What might I need to take time to simply sit with?

What lessons or insights did I gain through remembering my own or hearing of others' journeys?

Reflect upon the questions above and use the space below to journal your responses:

_____

_____

_____

_____

_____

Sexual Healing

1) If your loved one went through an illness or injury before their death, where did you see others losing sight of all he or she was?

_____

_____

_____

_____

2) We are more than the cause of our death. Sometimes, the diagnosis of a disease or a prognosis that our condition is terminal can become the primary focus of *who we are*, causing everyone to miss seeing the whole person. Did you ever feel the fullness of your loved one became lost in the crush of treatment details and symptom management?

_____

_____

_____

_____

3) What do you hope people will remember about your loved one?

_____

_____

_____

_____

_____

4) What will *you* remember most about them or your relationship together?

_____

_____

_____

_____

5) What dreams did your loved one complete before he or she died? Which were left undone?

_____

_____

_____

_____

6) What's on your bucket list? How does your experience of a loved one's death impact your sense of intention about working/experiencing that list?

_____

_____

_____

7) Have you ever experienced an inpatient hospice unit, aka hospice house? What was your impression of it?

_____

_____

_____

_____

8) If it applies to you, in what ways did you feel separated from your loved one by illness, injury, or the medical facility? What was that like for you?

_____

_____

_____

_____

ACTION PLAN:

Memories or thoughts arising from this story to hold onto…

Memories or thoughts arising from this story to let go of…

What action steps might I take to encourage my journey of grief further along?

What might I need to take time to simply sit with?

What lessons or insights did I gain through remembering my own or hearing of others' journeys?

Reflect upon the questions above and use the space below to journal your responses:

_____

_____

_____

_____

_____

_____

_____

_____

_____

Brazilian Dancer

1) How did you see denial occur surrounding the death you experienced?

_____

_____

_____

_____

2) What do you believe the role of denial is in protecting us in the early stages of grief?

_____

_____

_____

_____

3) Persons often want to die just as they have lived. In what ways did your loved one need to be heard? What did they need in order to die on their own terms? Was that able to happen for them?

_____

_____

_____

_____

4) Did your loved one ask for anything specific of you or others before they died that you know of? Was it something that was possible to provide? What was that like for you?

_____

_____

_____

_____

ACTION PLAN:

Memories or thoughts arising from this story to hold onto…

Memories or thoughts arising from this story to let go of…

What action steps might I take to encourage my journey of grief further along?

What might I need to take time to simply sit with?

What lessons or insights did I gain through remembering my own or hearing of others' journeys?

Reflect upon the questions above and use the space below to journal your responses:

_____

_____

_____

_____

_____

_____

_____

_____

_____

Two A.M. On-Call

1) What do you think of the idea that hearing and smell are the last senses to leave people at the end of life?

_____

_____

_____

2) How did the circumstances surrounding your loved one's death impact you? Was it for good or for ill? If there was something that complicated your grief, how have you tended to that? Is there more left to repair or heal?

_____

_____

_____

3) Consider the following quote from this story: "I believe we must help all disciplines and families better understand and recognize the necessity of tending to spiritual wounds as part of treating the whole person." Do you agree or disagree with this statement? Why or why not?

_____

_____

_____

4) What do you think made the difference for this man's peace of mind? Have you ever seen anyone struggling because of what seemed to be a spiritual or emotional wound? What was that like for you?

_____

_____

ACTION PLAN:

Memories or thoughts arising from this story to hold onto…

Memories or thoughts arising from this story to let go of…

What action steps might I take to encourage my journey of grief further along?

What might I need to take time to simply sit with?

What lessons or insights did I gain through remembering my own or hearing of others' journeys?

Reflect upon the questions above and use the space below to journal your responses:

_____

_____

_____

_____

_____

_____

_____

_____

_____

_____

_____

_____

_____

Only when you have made peace within yourself

will you be able to make peace in the world.

~Rabbi Simcha Bunim

Hank

1) What has been your experience of animals sensing your pain and responding to it?

_____

_____

_____

_____

2) What do you believe gets in our way of being as sensitive and responsive as Hank was in this story?

_____

_____

_____

_____

3) What thoughts get in the way or what rules do you think apply that keep us at a distance from others' pain?

_____

_____

_____

_____

4) What do you believe helps us just be with others when they are suffering without needing to fix it or avoid their pain?

_____

_____

_____

_____

5) Where have you found space(s) to just be with your feelings without someone needing to do anything other than just be with you in them?

_____

_____

_____

_____

ACTION PLAN:

Memories or thoughts arising from this story to hold onto…

Memories or thoughts arising from this story to let go of…

What action steps might I take to encourage my journey of grief further along?

What might I need to take time to simply sit with?

What lessons or insights did I gain through remembering my own or hearing of others' journeys?

Reflect upon the questions above and use the space below to journal your responses:

_____

_____

_____

_____

_____

Pet Therapy: My "Accidental" Discovery

1) What brought your loved one the most joy in his or her final days?

_____

_____

_____

_____

2) Consider the following quote from this story: "I'm glad the universe knew far better than I did what needed to happen." What does this statement mean to you?

_____

_____

_____

_____

3) Have you ever had an experience where you thought the universe or something greater than you took over? What happened? How do you understand it?

_____

_____

_____

_____

ACTION PLAN:

Memories or thoughts arising from this story to hold onto…

Memories or thoughts arising from this story to let go of…

What action steps might I take to encourage my journey of grief further along?

What might I need to take time to simply sit with?

What lessons or insights did I gain through remembering my own or hearing of others' journeys?

Reflect upon the questions above and use the space below to journal your responses:

_____

_____

_____

_____

_____

_____

_____

_____

_____

_____

_____

_____

_____

_____

Last Minute Forgiveness

1) How well were your loved one's wishes about aggressive or heroic measures known by others? What was that experience like for you?

_____

_____

_____

_____

2) Loved ones respond differently when a patient is dying. Some want to be present and close. Others want to let their last memory of the person they love to be when they were more alert or healthy, meaning they do not want to be there when the person dies. Where did you fall on that spectrum? What about your choices were helpful for you? Were any of your choices not helpful for you? Did others struggle with the choice of whether or not to be present around the time of death?

_____

_____

_____

_____

3) Which relationship in this story better characterizes your relationship with the person in your life who is now deceased—the closeness of the granddaughter and her mother or the polite distance of the patient and her daughter?

_____

_____

_____

4) Many do not have an experience of being able to heal old wounds with a person who is dying or has died. What was your experience? If there were things to heal, did you receive that healing? If so, how did it occur? If not, how does it still impact you?

_____

_____

_____

_____

ACTION PLAN:

Memories or thoughts arising from this story to hold onto…

Memories or thoughts arising from this story to let go of…

What action steps might I take to encourage my journey of grief further along?

What might I need to take time to simply sit with?

What lessons or insights did I gain through remembering my own or hearing of others' journeys?

Reflect upon the questions above and use the space below to journal your responses:

_____

_____

_____

_____

_____

_____

_____

_____

Suppressed grief suffocates, it rages within the breast, and is forced to multiply its strength.

~Ovid, Tristium, V, 1, 63.

Re-storying

1) What stories might you re-imagine about your loved one? The goal is not to deny reality, but to be open to seeing things in a different way that may be more helpful.

_____

_____

_____

_____

2) What are some stories about your loved one that work well just as they are, and that you find most meaningful?

_____

_____

_____

3) In what ways did you notice your loved one coping with illness or injury?

_____

_____

_____

4) Is there a way to reframe your view of suffering?

_____

_____

_____

5) What meaning, if any, have you found in the midst of your grief?

_____

_____

_____

_____

ACTION PLAN:

Memories or thoughts arising from this story to hold onto…

Memories or thoughts arising from this story to let go of…

What action steps might I take to encourage my journey of grief further along?

What might I need to take time to simply sit with?

What lessons or insights did I gain through remembering my own or hearing of others' journeys?

Reflect upon the questions above and use the space below to journal your responses:

_____

_____

_____

_____

_____

_____

_____

_____

_____

_____

We don't get past it. . . .

we learn to embrace it with our whole heart.

We don't move on . . .

we are carried by all the love around us.

We don't get stuck. . . .

we simply pause because this part

is harder to absorb.

We don't put it behind us . . .

we allow it to become part of who we are. . . . softening us into strength.

We don't forget . . .

we remember . . .

cherishing the deep gift of this loved one

~Janie Cook

Holding Space

1) If you had to choose between feeling abandoned by a lack of friends' presence or abandoned by their unhelpful words, which would you prefer? Which have you experienced?

_____

_____

_____

_____

2) When does it feel right to set boundaries with unhelpful words and when does it feel best to let them go?

_____

_____

_____

_____

3) How do we know when we are trying, needing, or wanting to be the hero and when we are being truly helpful?

_____

_____

_____

_____

_____

_____

4) Sometimes, the idea that gifts can come from pain is helpful and provides meaning for persons who are grieving. Other times, that idea feels hurtful or induces anger and frustration. How is that idea helpful or harmful for you?

_____

_____

_____

5) Consider the quote from this story: "Persons often fail to see the power they have by simply being with another in a compassionate way without needing to do anything more than that."

Is there someone who has been able to be present with you like this? Who is it? How does it feel to have (or not have) that safe space?

_____

_____

_____

6) Have you ever experienced someone beginning a comment to you with the words, "Well at least…"? What did they say? How did it feel? What would you have preferred they said?

_____

_____

_____

7) What would you like people to know about grieving the death of your loved one? What do you want them to understand about what it's like to be you?

_____

_____

_____

ACTION PLAN:

Memories or thoughts arising from this story to hold onto…

Memories or thoughts arising from this story to let go of…

What action steps might I take to encourage my journey of grief further along?

What might I need to take time to simply sit with?

What lessons or insights did I gain through remembering my own or hearing of others' journeys?

Reflect upon the questions above and use the space below to journal your responses:

_____

_____

_____

_____

_____

_____

_____

_____

_____

_____

_____

_____

_____

_____

_____

_____

_____

"*It's how we grow and heal, again and again, by holding and being held.*"

~Mark Nepo

Waking Up

1) What dynamics did you see in your family between in-town family members, family members directly involved in caring for your loved one, and out-of-town family members? Have you found peace with those dynamics? How have they changed your relationships for good or for ill? How have these things impacted your grief process?

---

2) Some feel they should have pushed harder or feel angry about what the medical team did or did not do. Such regrets can complicate the grief process as persons focus their anger on someone else, or with themselves, so much so that they can get stuck in the grieving process and not be able to move past it into peace and acceptance.

Anger is neither a good nor bad thing, as it gives us the energy we may need to push through the temporary depression that can occur during grief. Anger also gives us good information about things we may truly need to consider and/or do differently. But it may also distract us and cause more distress during the grief journey.

"What ifs" leave you grappling with yourself about your loved one's illness and death. These "If onlys" can be one way of bargaining or trying to feel more in control of an uncontrollable situation because it feels safer to believe we could have controlled or prevented tragedy. Where do you still lack peace that needs space to process? Which "what ifs" are you grappling with currently?

---

3) It is natural that some friendships will grow closer and stronger while others become more distant as we care for a loved one and/or grieve their death. This happens for many reasons. It can feel isolating to feel abandoned by family and friends. For others, it feels like a bit of a relief to have some space without feeling the need to tend to any other relationships or without having anyone else's input into how we are handling things.

What is/was your experience? How is/was it helpful or challenging to your journey?

_____

_____

_____

_____

4) The issue of Advance Directives and Do Not Resuscitate Orders can be hard for some families or family members. Many persons are clear that they want to be allowed to have a natural death, without aggressive intervention, when the time comes and it has been determined that they are not likely to recover easily or well. However, it can be difficult for family members to accept, respect, and abide by such decisions.

What was your experience with these conversations? What was it like for you to come to accept what your loved one wanted?

_____

_____

_____

_____

5) What is/was your experience of denial around your loved one's illness and/or death?

_____

_____

_____

_____

6) It can be much, much harder emotionally to stop an intervention, such as artificial respiration, hydration, or nutrition, once it has begun than to consent to never beginning it in the first place. Never starting it can feel like a benign act. Ending the intervention, even if it is appropriate medically, legally, and ethically, feels like a more active process that equates to killing the person.

Although this is not accurate, it often proves a challenge for family members. What was your experience with choices around starting or stopping interventions?

_____

_____

_____

_____

7) Were there ways in which your loved one's wishes (informally expressed or formalized as Advance Directives) were not upheld? If so, how has this affected your grief journey?

_____

_____

_____

_____

8) Grief is a process, not an event. Where did you find yourself impatient with your own, or others' process(es) of accepting a diagnosis or prognosis (the medical team's estimation about how quickly your loved one may decline and die)?

_____

_____

_____

_____

9) Where did you experience others being impatient with your process of coming to a place of acceptance?

10) What helped or hurt this process of coming to terms with reality?

11) One woman wrote that this story, and a couple of others in particular, helped her let go of how she wanted her mother's death to be so that her mother could experience the death she truly wanted and needed. Where did you find yourself grappling with what you wanted for your loved one versus what they wanted for themselves? How did you come to terms with that?

12) Based on your experience, how can a professional or team help someone break through reality without leading them to "dig in their heels" and without pushing them further than they are emotionally ready to go in finding acceptance?

ACTION PLAN:

Memories or thoughts arising from this story to hold onto…

Memories or thoughts arising from this story to let go of…

What action steps might I take to encourage my journey of grief further along?

What might I need to take time to simply sit with?

What lessons or insights did I gain through remembering my own or hearing of others' journeys?

Reflect upon the questions above and use the space below to journal your responses:

_____

_____

_____

_____

_____

_____

_____

_____

_____

_____

_____

_____

_____

If I Don't Say I'm Sorry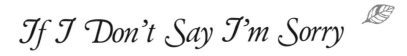

NOTE: I try to be clear throughout *Hospice Whispers: Stories of Life* and this corresponding workbook, as well as in my trainings and lectures, that this viewpoint is simply what helps *me* to do this work without overly worrying about others or carrying their sadness and grief with me to the point that I can no longer do my job.

It helps me to trust their process and trust them to find their way through. It also helps me remember not to try to take over the process that is theirs, and theirs alone.

I also try to be clear that I do not mean to impose such a view on those who are suffering, since I believe each person must find their own meaning. In the early, acute, stages of any of my grief experiences, someone suggesting that there may be "gifts" in my pain would have led me to want to scratch their eyeballs out on the spot!

These words were spoken from a position of trust and relationship. They were not hastily uttered, trite words followed by a fast retreat away from me and my pain; she was sitting with me in it and did not go away.

Over time, I found gifts unfolding for ME, and me alone. Each person will find meaning, peace, and comfort in their own way and such meaning should NEVER be imposed upon them.

So please hear me when I say I do not intend those suffering to take a Pollyannaish stance, to in any way minimize their grief experience, or even hint that I believe that suffering is caused for our good.

I hope that anyone who may misunderstand this story as my way of saying that their grief or suffering is a good thing will PLEASE hear that is NOT what I mean. Each person deserves to find their own way with their own values, without someone trying to spoon feed meaning to them. I simply hope that this will lead to helpful conversation rather than even more pain.

1) Some experience the words from my spiritual director in this story as harsh or unloving, while others hear them as caring and respectful (as I was thankfully able to hear them). What is your reaction to them?

_____

_____

_____

_____

_____

2) Where have you seen growth in your life as a result of any of the suffering you have experienced?

_____

_____

_____

_____

3) Some take comfort in believing a deity has caused suffering while others do not. What is your view and what about it helps or hurts you?

_____

_____

_____

_____

4) What brings you peace in the midst of your grief? How, if at all, do you make sense of suffering? If you have no answers, what helps you accept that unknown?

_____

_____

_____

_____

5) "Experience has taught me that something I believed at one time was the best thing in the world can change into a difficulty in a second, and the things I most resented in the moment often resulted in some of my greatest gifts."

What does this quote mean to you?

_____

_____

_____

I want to become porous

for life, love, pain and joy to flow through me

effortlessly

constantly

blessing each breath

I want to take the brittle

inflexible pieces of my life

people of my life

and carefully, delicately,

loosely

weave them together

until they flow

softly

as one

constant

gift

~Janie Cook

ACTION PLAN:

Memories or thoughts arising from this story to hold onto…

Memories or thoughts arising from this story to let go of…

What action steps might I take to encourage my journey of grief further along?

What might I need to take time to simply sit with?

What lessons or insights did I gain through remembering my own or hearing of others' journeys?

Reflect upon the questions above and use the space below to journal your responses:

_____

_____

_____

_____

_____

_____

_____

_____

_____

_____

_____

_____

_____

_____

The Queen

NOTE: I've learned from readers' feedback that we all have that one story that grabs us. This one is mine. It was the last story I wrote for the book, and it's the last story I'm writing these questions for, because it is the closest and dearest to my heart, as well as the hardest. I miss her, still. I hope The Queen teaches you as much as she taught me.

1) This story begins with a discussion of boundaries and caregiving in a way that is all about the other person, rather than what we want or need to happen. It can be far easier to hold these boundaries in a professional setting, when we are more emotionally removed from a person or situation.

But it can also be helpful to hold similar boundaries in our personal lives, so that we do not interfere in the process another person needs to have—a dignity of autonomy they deserve, and also so that we do not over-function, take on too much, and wear ourselves out.

Where did you see yourself possibly taking on more than was fair, to you or others, in your circumstance? What did you learn from this experience that might help you grow to a deeper place in your daily life about letting go and giving persons space to have their own experience?

_____

_____

_____

_____

2) Where did you find yourself identifying with the person who was dying? How did that impact your experience of feeling for or sympathizing with what they were going through?

_____

_____

_____

_____

3) Some deaths involve an element of the other shoe dropping. For some, they finally retire to travel with their spouse, but then find out they are ill. For others, it's beating cancer, or another diagnosis, just to have it return with a vengeance. Many struggle with what they perceive to be the unfairness of such stories.

How do you make sense of or find meaning in such existential (questions of existence) struggles?

_____

_____

_____

_____

4) Again, we see the issue of unresolved problems and unhealed relationships, which can be hard to accept. What was left unresolved for you with your loved one? How well have you found peace with that? What else can you do to find peace, even if the outcome will never be exactly as you wanted?

_____

_____

_____

_____

5) What do you think of as a good death? How do you reconcile that what you need and want may not be what others need and want? Where have you found space to make room for differences without some having to be right while others are wrong? Where is it still hard for you?

_____

_____

_____

Tenderness is strength, never weakness.

True courage is found

in letting ourselves be vulnerable.

~Flavia

ACTION PLAN:

Memories or thoughts arising from this story to hold onto…

Memories or thoughts arising from this story to let go of…

What action steps might I take to encourage my journey of grief further along?

What might I need to take time to simply sit with?

What lessons or insights did I gain through remembering my own or hearing of others' journeys?

Reflect upon the questions above and use the space below to journal your responses:

_____

_____

_____

_____

_____

_____

_____

_____

_____

_____

_____

_____

_____

_____

_____

To Be Clear

Are there ways in which you feel somehow inadequate or still hold regrets from how you handled your particular situation? How might you let go of those feelings of inadequacy and accept that you did the best you could at the time with the information you had in the circumstance you faced? How might you learn from those moments when you feel you were not your best self so as to transform what seems like a negative into something beneficial?

Some persons find that ritual can be helpful to choose a different way to see or feel about something from the past that cannot be changed. Writing a list of regrets and putting them into a G-d box or burning it or scattering it to the wind or on the water is a way that many have found to let go.

Find whatever feels right for you, but please find something. A loved one has died. It is done. And decisions get made during times of stress based on instinct and the best information we have. We get to let ourselves off the hook for being imperfect.

Certainly, if damage was done to someone else and true guilt is present over not acting as you normally prefer to with others, then it can be a very healing and freeing thing to make amends. Apologize, without excuse. Simply say, "I'm sorry, I hope you'll forgive me," or, "How can we make things right again?" This is a scary but important process which is good not just for them, but also for you!

Find a way to free yourself from judgments—others' and your own. If shame is hovering around, bring it into the light. Shame loves dark corners to hide in. Brene Brown has some fabulously helpful and well-researched concepts regarding shame, vulnerability, and authenticity.

From her writings, which include: *The Gifts of Imperfection, Daring Greatly,* and *Rising Strong* to her speaking at either of her TED Talks or on her audiobook, *The Power of Vulnerability,* Brene's wisdom may help you find healing and hope in areas where you are being held captive by the past.

Again, if you've been working through this workbook alone and find struggles coming up that may need more support than words on a page can provide, please contact a local hospice and ask about grief counseling services available in your area. Find safe spaces for your emotions to breathe and feel heard and accepted, rather than be judged. Find places where you can talk until you can hear yourself, and make more sense out of what you have experienced and find yourself experiencing, still.

As we come toward the end of this workbook, hear the closing words once again from the piece "To Be Clear" as it was first introduced in *Hospice Whispers: Stories of Life*:

"This book was intended to point to the rich gifts and experiences that punctuate what seems to the outside world as an impossibly sad job. My hope was to make death seem a little less scary, to make hospice just a little better understood, to help families and even patients feel just a little more prepared for what the process can look like.

But to be clear, it ain't always puppies and ponies. I am good at what I do, but I am by no means the best or wisest chaplain I know. This book isn't intended to be a made for television movie in which the ending is all neatly tied up with a delicate bow. So please, do not hold yourself as a patient, family, or professional caregiver to a standard that isn't real. We look for the gifts and beauty and perfection in the midst of all the messy imperfection and seek to learn from it all—the seemingly 'good' and the seemingly 'bad.'

As artist, Salvador Dali said, 'Have no fear of perfection—you'll never reach it.' Thankfully, we do not need to."

ACTION PLAN:
Memories or thoughts arising from this story to hold onto…
Memories or thoughts arising from this story to let go of…
What action steps might I take to encourage my journey of grief further along?
What might I need to take time to simply sit with?
What lessons or insights did I gain through remembering my own or hearing of others' journeys?

Reflect upon the questions above and use the space below to journal your responses:

_____

_____

_____

_____

_____

_____

_____

_____

_____

_____

_____

Already Inside of You

1) What from this book rings true for you? Can you see ways in which the information here isn't necessarily new, but has helped you to recognize what you already know to be true?

_____

_____

_____

_____

2) What of this book does not ring true for you? Are you able to either reframe those things and/or let them go?

_____

_____

_____

_____

3) If you were to add anything to this book to help others, both lay persons and professionals, what would it be?

_____

_____

_____

_____

_____

4) How has your trust in your own wisdom grown over the course of engaging with the workbook material?

_____

_____

_____

_____

ACTION PLAN:

Memories or thoughts arising from this story to hold onto…

Memories or thoughts arising from this story to let go of…

What action steps might I take to encourage my journey of grief further along?

What might I need to take time to simply sit with?

What lessons or insights did I gain through remembering my own or hearing of others' journeys?

**Reflect upon the questions above and use the space below to journal your responses:**

_____

_____

_____

_____

_____

_____

_____

_____

_____

_____

Now,

it is as if I breathe Matt . . . in and out.

His words are the wind blowing in the trees he loved,

    the bird songs he could whistle so perfectly,

    the infinite colors of wildflowers

    and the brilliance of butterflies darting in and out of sight.

Our conversations are different, but

    I feel him with me

    and "know" what he is urging me

    to do,

    to be,

    to enjoy.

It is a stunning thing

    to let go of the dependence upon the "outer covering"

    and relish the radiance of his constant presence.

                -Janie Cook

She was no longer wrestling with the grief,

but could sit down with it as a lasting companion

and make it a sharer in her thoughts.

~George Eliot

Acknowledgments

Tremendous thanks to:

Amy Kappler, the artist who first created the Hospice Whispers necklace and helped me pick it out in her booth at the Pecan Street Arts Festival in 2006. Six years later, she heard my vision and passion as I began leading trainings for healthcare staff. She graciously said, "Yes!" to allowing the necklace image to become my business logo…then the *Hospice Whispers: Stories of Life* book cover…now it is the cover for this workbook. She has even recreated the original necklace so others may enjoy it, as well. Your generosity is as great as your talent.

Laura Saintey, for her beautiful acrylic painting of the necklace that still shines and glimmers mysteriously over me as I write at my desk, and for being a true "sis" who believes in and shares her gifts with me.

Laura Jenkins, who crafted that painting into the original front cover graphic design, encourages my writing with her own beautiful words, and remains a constant member of my chosen spiritual family.

The contributors who originally shared their stories in *Hospice Whispers: Stories of Life*: Joan Kingery, RN, Rev. Dr. Rodney Bolejack, and Bernadette Noll, whose words now contribute to even more healing.

Mindy Reed, Danielle Acee, Rebecca Byrd Arthur, and Danylle Salinas from The Authors' Assistant for their on-going guidance, insight, and encouragement.

The many advance readers who brought their hearts and minds to bear on this project, gifting me with the benefit of their personal and professional experiences. Their feedback helped to refine this workbook so it may be as beneficial as possible both for those grieving and the volunteers and clinicians who seek to support them.

And to Janie Cook, friend and colleague, who courageously said, "Yes" when I asked to share her hard-earned wisdom of grief in the tender words of her poetry that grace these pages.

To all of these, and more, we will never find a big enough word, but so long as we try to do so…

Thank you!

About the Author

Rev. Dr. Carla Cheatham began her career in social services with an MA in Psychology, certification in trauma counseling, and experience working in child and family therapy services and substance abuse treatment centers. She taught and researched on the interaction between spirituality and health at Texas A&M while receiving her PhD in Health & Kinesiology and earned her M.Div. with an award from the Charles and Elizabeth Perkins Prothro Fellowship at Southern Methodist University's Perkins School of Theology.

After serving faith communities and directing an interfaith non-profit supporting worker justice, Carla began her work as a hospice chaplain and bereavement coordinator in Austin, Texas.

She is the Principal and Lead Trainer for Carla Cheatham Consulting Group, LLC and serves as a national and keynote speaker and consultant for end of life care teaching around boundaries and healthy teams, ethical spiritual and existential care, and grief support.

Carla is the Section Leader for the National Hospice and Palliative Care Organization's Spiritual Caregivers Section, a member of NHPCO's Ethics Advisory Committee, serves on the Board of Directors for Swan Songs, a non-profit that fulfills end of life musical wishes, and is an Adjunct Professor teaching about Hospice and Palliative Care at the Seminary of the Southwest.

She is the author of *Hospice Whispers: Stories of Life* and its companion piece, *Sharing Our Stories: A Hospice Whispers Grief Support Workbook*, both available through Amazon.

Her next book on the art of presence with those who are suffering is set for publication in 2017. Carla is a guest blogger for hospicetimes.com, and publishes her own blog at carlacheatham.com/carlas-blog/ and her blog through hospicewhispers.com.

Learn more about Carla's speaking at carlacheatham.com and her writings, Hospice Whispers necklace, and other products at hospicewhispers.com

Made in the USA
Middletown, DE
24 February 2017